Tragic Time in Drama, Film, and Videogames

Rebecca Bushnell

Tragic Time in Drama, Film, and Videogames

The Future in the Instant

Rebecca Bushnell
Department of English
University of Pennsylvania
Philadelphia, Pennsylvania, USA

ISBN 978-1-137-58525-7   ISBN 978-1-137-58526-4 (eBook)
DOI 10.1057/978-1-137-58526-4

Library of Congress Control Number: 2016952877

Cover illustration: Pattern adapted from an Indian cotton print produced in the 19th century

Printed on acid-free paper

This Palgrave Macmillan imprint is published by Springer Nature
The registered company is Macmillan Publishers Ltd.
The registered company address is: The Campus, 4 Crinan Street, London, N1 9XW, United Kingdom

PREFACE

In the videogame *The Stanley Parable*, the player inhabits an avatar named Stanley, who punches computer buttons all day. A soothing voice with a British accent begins the game with a past-tense narration, telling the player that one day Stanley found himself unaccountably alone. The player starts by moving in concert with the narration, and, acting as Stanley, emerges from an office to seek his absent colleagues. She thus embarks on an adventure, the nature of which depends on choices made along the way. The narrator leads the player early on to a room where one must choose which door to enter, the left or the right. The narrator says Stanley entered the left one, but in the present of the game the player can also open the right door, in effect disobeying the narrator. If the player chooses the left door and conforms with the narration throughout the short story, as Stanley she can escape the office building and its "mind-control machine." The player will be told Stanley was now "free" and that he was "happy." If the player disobeys the narrator at any point, those choices can lead to many different endings, where Stanley might die, stay in a broom closet, get lost in an infinite loop, go mad, or even enter another game, among many other options.[1]

The Stanley Parable thus not only parodies the mechanisms of choice that underlie most videogames but also exposes a fundamental tension at the heart of tragedy: that is, the conflict between a narrative's drive toward a satisfying conclusion and its need to imply that characters are free to make choices—however terrible and self-destructive. *The Stanley Parable* teaches the player that making the choices the narrator proposes may seem to "free" you but only because you have conformed with the program;

disobedience means death or never finding your way to the end. It also starkly demonstrates the conflict between the player's experience of the game in real time, in the present, and the narrator's desperately trying to keep the narrative in the past tense. The player's disobedience constantly drags the narrator to fight with the player in the present where the player can assert his or her freedom—at whatever cost.

This book aims at the heart of the problem that *The Stanley Parable* poses, which is also central to the genre of tragedy: how we experience choice and consequences in time, and especially in an enacted present that conflicts with the past. This book is based on the premise that tragedy is not dead: rather, it lives in new forms, and especially in contemporary media like videogames and films that stage the mechanics of causality and necessity. Many books have been written on the subject of tragedy and its relationship to modern life, especially concerning the representation of violence and suffering in new media culture. But this book explores instead how theatre and tragedy have shaped the representation of time and the consequences of action in multiple media, and in turn, how those new media have reframed the temporality of tragedy.

This book thus participates in the recent "turn to time" in literary and cultural studies, which has brought people to question common assumptions about how time works, whether it be in history, culture, or lived experience. Some attribute this scholarly turn to the exhaustion of the new historicism. More broadly, it also reflects a reaction against how linear time has been used to define how we live in the mind, body, and world.[2] Critics have produced a lot of work on temporality in literature, but much of it, including Mikhail Bakhtin's influential theorizing of the chronotope, Peter Brook's *Reading for the Plot*, Gérard Genette's *Narrative Discourse*, and Paul Ricoeur's magisterial three-volume work on *Time and Narrative*, has focused on the novel rather than theater. My own concern is the temporality of *enacted* stories, not just texts, and not just with how time is represented, but with how it is experienced by players and audiences alike.

Often when scholars write about time they are really talking about something else, like "mutability" or "history." Of course, it is hard to think about time except as it is embodied *in* something else: in matter, nature, or human behavior and events.[3] Stephen Toulmin and June Goodfield have narrated the human discovery of time through observing change: first in the "changes and chances of individual human life" but then also in the course of human affairs and "the mutability of the Earth, the living creatures upon it, and even the great Heavens themselves" (21).

But buried in this identification of time with change is the broader question of how to define time itself: in Dan Falk's words, "Is time nothing more than change? Or is time more fundamental—is it the mysterious entity that *makes change possible*, a kind of foundation on which the universe is built?" (272).

Switching from thinking about change to instead describing the experience of time brings us to the mystery of what it means to live in the present. Falk wonders what happens if we question the sense of time as a river, asking "could the river be dry, its flow an illusion […] If the flow is imaginary, have 'past' and 'future' dried up along with it, leaving only an array of 'nows,' all on an equal footing?" (73). The idea of the urgency of the present time is not a new one: Martin Luther once wrote, drawing on St. Augustine, "What the philosophers say is true: 'The past is gone; the future has not arrived; therefore we have, of all time, only the now. The rest of time is not because it has either passed away or has not yet arrived'" (cited in Waller 19).[4] One could see this early conception of time as paralleling the modern conception of time in physics, understood not as linear flow but rather as "a vast block in which past and future have equal status. 'Now,' meanwhile, is reduced to a subjective label, just like 'here'" (Falk 4).

This book does not delve deeply into the philosophy or physics of time. Rather, I focus more narrowly on the ways in which theater, films, and videogames enact the experience of living in a sense of present time that cannot be disentangled from the past and future.[5] Although I began studying time in classical and Renaissance tragedy years ago, the shape of this particular book has been influenced by my rereading tragedy after watching time-travel films and playing videogames.[6] In each chapter, I will contend that when it comes to temporality, the medium matters: the enacted media of theater, film, and videogames all engage the spectator—and the player—differently in time. Time-travel films first brought my attention to how filmmakers have used the unique qualities of their medium to undo necessity as it is embedded in linear time, taking advantage of film's ability to "time travel." But more than anything else, playing serious videogames has deeply complicated how I understand the mechanisms of tragic necessity and the tragic protagonist's actions in time.

In *Hamlet on the Holodeck*, a seminal study of what was still a new medium in 1998, Janet Murray argued that in videogames "the interactor is the author of a particular performance within an electronic story system, or the architect of a particular part of the virtual world, but we must distinguish this derivative authorship from the originating authorship of the system itself [...] This is not authorship but agency" (153). This tension between the "authorship" of the system and the player's role as author of his or her own performance parallels the conflict between the power that we want to call "fate" and the tragic actor/protagonist's acting as a self with an ability to choose. Critical to any videogame is how the player is given freedom to choose and act in the context of an unfolding story, while the extent to which those decisions matter in the end can be quite different. On the one hand, videogames seem to grant a player significant "authorship" through the ability to determine a course of action at selected moments: to kill or not kill an antagonist, to forgive or reject a partner. In so doing, a player may affect the shape of the plot in process or even its outcome. For many game theorists, this kind of agency is, after all, what makes a game a game as opposed to a text, play, or film. As Jesper Juul has noted, because the game players are the actors, single-player games make them deeply complicit, feeling responsible for the story's outcome (Juul 2013 [location 452]).

Videogames have thus brought me to look at tragic theater in the context of games and play.[7] Some may see such an approach as counter-intuitive: surely, games and play suggest comedy, a world of experimentation and possibility rather than the closed-down world of tragedy, where everything seems to be predetermined. But I am using game thinking to open up what appears to be closed in tragedy, seeking ways in which tragic theater could approximate the conditions of play. I am adapting Roger Caillois's description of play as an activity defined by six essential qualities: play is voluntary; "separate" or "circumscribed within limits of space and time"; unproductive; make-believe; governed by rules that "suspend ordinary laws"; and for me, most importantly "uncertain," insofar as its course "cannot be determined, nor the result attained beforehand, and some latitude for innovation [is] left to the player's initiative" (9–10).[8] Further connecting the idea of play to videogames, I argue that understanding how videogames function can unlock the possibilities and play latent in tragedy, both in theater and in film. When videogames adapt generic formulas derived from this theatrical tradition, they also uncover what was always there, temporal contingencies and hypotheses that can exist within a traditional play's "program."[9]

It might by now be obvious that, for me, writing this short book meant traveling into new territories: theories and philosophy of time, performance studies, film theory, and game studies. While I think this book responsibly represents my investigations in the different disciplines involved, above all it is meant to be accessible to people from all those fields. Thus, my goal is not necessarily to add great depth in the special areas of these individual disciplines: for example, the classical scholar might find the coverage of the vast literature on *Oedipus the King* scanty, and in turn, the film scholar might expect much more detailed work on cinematic time. Instead, I hope that scholars from all these fields—literature, theatre, film, gaming—might learn something from looking at their discipline from another perspective. The book is designed to encourage conversation among people in different areas, for example, by asking game scholars to think about theatrical performance and students of tragedy to try their hand at a serious game.

In several ways, this project entailed some deviation from recent scholarly trends in my own area of literary and cultural studies. First, because it covers many kinds of "performance" from different periods, I am sailing recklessly through the powerful wake of thirty years of historicism in early modern studies. While I have long recognized history's claims, in thinking about tragedy I am resisting here the idea that time moves only in one continuous direction. Rather, following Michel Serres and others, I want to think that "every historical era is multi-temporal, simultaneously drawing from the obsolete, the contemporary and the futuristic" (Serres 60). I am indeed concerned with how the past both differs from and informs the present, but I also see that the present can make us rethink or reconstruct the past.[10] I concur with Rita Felski's argument against using context or periodization as a straitjacket, where we are "impaled on the pin of our historical categories and coordinates," in which a text "exists only as an object-to-be-explained rather than a fellow actor and cocreator of relations, attitudes, and attachments" (509–10).

This book may also seem to veer out of the critical mainstream because it makes claims about a genre called tragedy. Genre criticism has often been held in disrepute, largely because much of it has focused defining genres and policing their boundaries, a project so ably deconstructed by Jacques Derrida in his essay on "The Law of Genre."[11] However, this book is not concerned with those kind of definitions. When discussing time-travel films or videogames, I will not address the question of whether they are tragedies: that is not the point. Instead, I am asserting that over the long haul, enacted tragedies have established expectations for representing and experiencing events in time, in many performative media.[12]

As loosely identified with a collection of texts, a genre establishes what Hans Robert Jauss called the "objectifiable system of expectations that arises for each work in the historical moment of its appearance" (22).[13] But that is certainly not a stable system; Jauss argues that throughout time, even as something like the idea of a genre as "tragedy" persists, those expectations shift, as each "new text evokes for the reader (listener) the horizon of expectation and 'rules of the game' familiar to him from earlier texts." Yet, in turn, these "rules" can be "varied, extended, corrected, but also transformed, crossed out, or simply reproduced" (88). That is, a genre is like a game, constantly in the process of dynamic change, where the new adapts the old, but in so doing also transforms the way we see the old. In proposing that we think about cultural production in the context of "deep time," Wai-Chee Dimock also asks us to see genre developing not merely in a linear fashion but rather as "a set of longitudinal frames, at once projective and recessional, with input going both ways, and binding continents and millennia into many loops of relations, a densely interactive fabric" (3–4). So here I am exploring how modern performance, adaptations, film, and videogames expose and transform the deep structure of tragic temporality, with "input going both ways."

This book may also raise some critical eyebrows in its unabashed focus on freedom, agency, and choice. At times when writing this book I felt like I must sound like an unreconstructed 1950s existentialist, uninformed by or even unaware of the last thirty years of cultural and political criticism that has thoroughly complicated and undermined all of these concepts. In fact, all of my scholarship in the past has been in dialogue with this criticism. My first book, *Prophesying Tragedy: Sign and Voice in Sophocles' Theban Plays*, tackled some of the same questions I address here, in considering the tragic hero's resistance to entrapment in his own story as represented in the future language of prophecy. In that book I followed the tragic heroes' ethical drive to reject or subvert prophecy, that is, to write their own stories, but I concluded that, of course, they could not do so in the end, because "their stories belong to everyone, not to themselves alone" (107). I took the position then, as I do now, that we should not take the idea of tragic "fate" for granted; I was guided by Walter Benjamin's wise statement on tragedy that "The necessity which appears to be built into the framework is neither a causal nor a magical necessity. It is the unarticulated necessity of defiance, in which the self brings forth its utterances" (115). As I look back over my thirty-five years of scholarship since then, I recognize that I have never stopped writing about cultural forms of resistance to authority, whether embodied in prophecy, tyranny, pedagogy, or even gardening. Rather than starting with a pre-existing theoretical framework, I always tried first to understand that discourse on its own terms and then to engage in dialogue with contemporary theory. Here I have taken another approach by thinking about choice, agency, and authorship in terms adapted from game studies, but it always with an eye to the specific qualities of different media.[14]

The primary concern of much game studies theory has been the function of interactivity, which negotiates a complex balance between "free choice" and the purposes of a game. Mark Wolf has described how choice and consequence work in videogames:

> The very 'rules' and cause-and-effect logic that dictate the events of the video game's diegetic world contain an imbedded world view which matches actions with consequences and determines outcomes, and it is here that an author can best guide a player into a particular way of thinking (and acting). Goals and obstacles, choices and their consequences, and the means and ends with which the player is provided; these become the tools that shape narrative experience, and the real narrative becomes the player's own passage through the narrative maze of branching storylines and events. (*Medium* 109)[15]

Thus one could say that, like a tragedy, a game has a story to tell in which "free" choice becomes an essential part of its framework, or in Espen Aarseth's words, a structural feature of "the prison-house of regulated play" (133).[16] Thus, while the player feels involved in the present of play when she is free to choose, in the end all of her choices are part of the plan. But videogames, of course, differ most significantly from the conventional view of tragedy in offering multiple choices in the present. In this sense, playing videogames exposes how tragic ends are constructed in time. It has brought me to look again for the multiple stories latent in any tragic script, in what *Macbeth* calls the "seeds of time."

In order to establish the grounds of its argument, this book begins by considering the temporality of classical and Shakespearean tragedy, offering readings of a select set of plays meant to unsettle conventional ideas about how choice relates to both tragic character and consequences. I then discuss how performance and adaptation can uncover the temporal contingencies underlying tragic narratives, using the case studies of Tom Stoppard's *Rosencrantz and Guildenstern Are Dead* and The Performance

Group's historic production of *Dionysus in 69*. The book then turns to the ways in which time-travel films can challenge the linearity that we associate with tragic present time. This chapter pursues the implications of the time-travel film's investment in film's multifaceted temporality, and with that questions how time can be manipulated to open up new ends. Only then do I get to videogames, exploring in the final chapter how videogames make us rethink the tragic time that is defined by the "end." In fact, the book was written backward, beginning with my playing and then writing about games. That experience in turn informed my rethinking of the plays, performances, and films I discuss. When I finally came to compose the first chapter on classical and Renaissance tragedy, my way of reading the dramatic tradition thus was transformed by my experience of serious play, seeing how choice and consequences work in present time. If a reader chooses to read the book backward as well, that is fine with me.

Writing this book has been a wonderful adventure, but as I travelled into unfamiliar territory, I depended on having knowledgeable and kindly guides who tolerated my naiveté and steered me in the right direction. Phyllis Rackin first suggested that I write a book about time and tragedy, and as always, I thank her for her wisdom and friendship. Since then, many colleagues and students have been teaching me about those fields in which I was a novice, and I apologize that I cannot possibly remember or name them all here. However, I am particularly grateful to the Cinema Studies faculty at Penn (especially Timothy Corrigan and Karen Beckman), as well as friends and colleagues with expertise in theatre and performance (including Cary Mazer, Erika Lin, and Gina Bloom). Matthew Wagner's book and his collegiality have both been inspirational. But I owe the greatest debt for this book to my daughter Ruth Bushnell Toner. Professionally Ruth is a data scientist but she is also a dedicated gamer who first made me the importance of videogames for the study of choice and consequences. She also taught me how to play them myself and let me watch her shoot and navigate her way through many game worlds. This work has greatly benefited from her insights and encouragement; it is really partly hers. Of course, I also am grateful to my husband John Toner and my daughter Emily Bushnell Toner, for their love, kindness, and tolerance of my insistence on watching cheesy time-travel films. I also want to thank Ben Doyle for encouraging me to write this book for Palgrave Pivot, when it was just a wild idea, and Bronwyn Wallace, for her incisive comments and her patient help in preparing the manuscript.

Some material from the book has appeared in an earlier form in a short essay on "Tragedy and Temporality," *PMLA* 129 (2014), 783–789.

NOTES

1. See, for example, Fenner, "The Stanley Parable Endings Guide" (Fenner 2013).

2. For examples of recent work on time and literature in areas closest to my own field of early modern studies: Newman et al., *Time and the Literary*; Wood, *Time, Narrative, and Emotion*; Harris, *Untimely Matter*; Wagner, *Shakespeare, Theatre, and Time*; Fletcher, *Time, Space, and Motion in the Age of Shakespeare*; Cohen, *Medieval Identity Machines*; Dinshaw, *How Soon is Now?* See Lewis for a review of the history of criticism on Shakespeare and temporality; also Cohen, Chap. 1, on "critical temporal studies." Temporality has also been a focus of significant recent work in queer studies: see Dinshaw 32–33 for a summary of this work with a bibliography (Dinshaw 2012).

3. Over the period I've been concerned with this project, I have consulted many general books on time and temporality (in addition to the works cited in note 2), and many specific studies of temporality and tragedy, theater, film, and videogames are covered in Chaps. 1–4. Here I will just mention three older books that traditionally shaped thinking about time in Western culture since the Middle Ages: Quinones, *The Renaissance Discovery of Time*; Waller, *The Strong Necessity of Time*; and Kermode, *The Sense of an Ending*. Toulmin and Goodfield, *The Discovery of Time*, and Falk, *In Search of Time*, provide useful summaries of the issues for a general reader. The essays in Burges and Elias, *Time: A Vocabulary of the Present*, offer a comprehensive survey of theories of temporality focused the post Second World War world. My own general thinking about temporality has been influenced by Serres, *Conversations on Science, Culture and Time*, and Hoy, *The Time of our Lives*, and I have benefitted greatly from Wagner's phenomenological approach in *Shakespeare, Theatre, and Time*. However, mostly I have focused on the temporality of the individual media I discuss rather than general theories of time.

4. See also Waller on Michel de Montaigne: "He finds it impossible to pin down the essence of man except in the present instant: 'I describe not the essence,' he exclaims, 'but the passage; not a passage from age to age, or as people reckon, from seaven years to seaven, but from day to day, from minute to minute'" (30).

5. See Hoy on "a conceptual distinction between the terms 'time' and 'temporality.' The term 'time' can be used to refer to universal time, clock time, or objective time. In contrast, 'temporality' is time insofar as it manifests itself in human existence" (xiii). I will not be so rigorous in distinguishing between the two terms (Hoy 2012).

6. Throughout this book my observations are limited to single-player rather than multiplayer games.

7. See Bloom 126 for a review of recent work on games and early modern theater. Much of my approach here has been influenced by Richard Schechner's *Performance Theory*.

8. Of course, there are other scholars who have argued that we take the idea of play seriously and even when it comes to tragedy: for example, the classic work by anthropologist Victor Turner, *From Ritual to Theatre: The Human Seriousness of Play*, more recently Alexander Riley, *Impure Play*. Paul Armstrong has also produced important work on the theories of play, narrative, and reading: see Arnstrong, *Play and the Politics of Reading*, and *How Literature Plays with the Brain*.

9. See Morson, *Narrative and Freedom*, for an in-depth consideration of these issues, albeit focused on the novel. See also Simon Palfrey, *Shakespeare's Possible Worlds*. Palfrey's interest is similar to mine, in that he sees that in Shakespeare "we seem never to be given something—word, concept, emotion, institution—without being asked to imagine it otherwise, inside out, upside down, con-joined" (33) (Palfrey 2014); however, our methodological approaches are very different, and my emphasis is on action and the effects of choice in time. At the last minute in writing this book I discovered Daniel Sack's excellent *After Live: Possibility, Potentiality and Performance*. This book explores the potentiality, "a withheld realization, a possession of the capacity to do or develop" (9), latent in live performance, which is also a theme of this book (Sack 2015). However, Sack's emphasis is more on contemporary theater practice.

10. In this sense, I sympathize with Marjorie Garber's premise that "Shakespeare makes modern culture and modern culture makes Shakespeare" (1) (Garber 2008). This book shares some concerns with the critical approach called "presentism," as defined by DiPietro and Grady in *Shakespeare and the Urgency of Now*: "an approach to the past based on a self-conscious position of the perceiver in the present, aware of historical difference but aware as well of the approach-able but real epistemological barrier between ourselves and the past—and deliberately choosing to highlight our presentness, whether as a methodological starting point, the inevitable horizon of interpretation, or its enabling condi-tion" (4) (DiPietro and Grady 2013).

11. See Dimock, "Genres"; see also Frow, *Genre*, Chap. 1; Altman, *Film/Genre*, Chap. 1; also Robbins, who notes that "when genre is discussed, the metaphor of the police is everywhere" (1646) (Robbins 2007).

12. See also Dubrow, *Genre*, on "genre as a code of behavior established between the author and his reader" (2) (Dubrow 1982); Colie, *Resources of Kind*, writes of the way in which "patterns, kinds, mental sets organize for us the lives we individually lead, much as kind, sets, patterns organized the vast body of literature" (30) (Colie 1974).

13. See also Dimock, "Genres": "Far from being clear-cut slices of the literary pie, genres have only an on-demand spatial occupancy. They can be brought forth or sent back as the user chooses, switched on or off, scaled up or down" (1379) (Dimock 2007).

14. Another interesting context for this discussion has been the recent explosion in studies of choice and decision-making in the social sciences. See Orr on the importance of choice in the American consciousness, which has generated vast numbers of popular self-help books about how to make better decisions. Some of the current literature on choice in behavioral economics focuses on the ways in which those moments of choosing in the flash of time may draw on intuition or unconscious thinking; see Malcolm Gladwell's *Blink* on intuitive thinking and Daniel Kahneman's *Thinking Fast and Slow* on the hazards of such "fast thinking." But this social science work is mostly focused on how people approach choice with regard to short-term rather than long-term consequences, what is known as "intertemporal choice": for example, see Lowenstein et al., *Time and Decision.*

15. See also Smethurst and Craps: "In order to acknowledge the fact that during gameplay, it is not only the game that reacts to the player but also the player who reacts to the game, we amalgamate interactivity and reactivity into a third term: interreactivity" (273) (Smethurst and Craps 2015).

16. Bogost follows how videogames function as a form of "procedural rhetoric": "the art of persuasion through rule-based representations and interactions," that is, as a way of making a point, or making something happen, through the gamer's experience of a sequence of procedures (ix). So in this context, "choices are selectively included and excluded in a procedural representation to procure a desired expressive end" (45) (Bogost 2010).

CONTENTS

Contents

CHAPTER 1

Time, Choice, and Consequences in Greek and Shakespearean Tragedy

Abstract This chapter focuses on how classical and Shakespearean tragedy engages us in a present "thick" with past and future when it stages a crisis, a moment of present decision in which everything changes. It argues that understanding tragic temporality as multidirectional than merely linear opens up new ways of thinking about how choice operates in present time. The chapter analyzes the relationship of choice in time to character and consequences in a small set of plays: Aeschylus's *Oresteia*, Sophocles's Theban plays, and Shakespeare's *Macbeth* and *Hamlet*, which have served as powerful paradigms for the construction of tragic temporality and crisis. The chapter's first part concerns the relationship between choice and dramatic character, considering how tragic character can be defined through choice, anticipating the deconstruction of character formation that takes place in videogames. The second part also questions the assumption that the tragic protagonist's decision is constrained by the power that human beings have called the gods, fate, or destiny. Positing that the present moment of decision may still be radically contingent, this chapter asserts that in Greek and Shakespearean tragedy choice in an enacted crisis can undermine as well as reinforce the kind of determinism that we conventionally associate with those plays.

Keywords Time · Temporality · Choice · Tragedy · Drama · Character · Fate · Prophecy · *Oresteia* · Sophocles · Aeschylus · *Oedipus the King* · Oedipus · *Antigone* · Play · Games · Shakespeare · *Hamlet* · *Macbeth*

© The Author(s) 2016
R. Bushnell, *Tragic Time in Drama, Film, and Videogames*,
DOI 10.1057/978-1-137-58526-4_1

1

It has become common to think that tragic time is "now," binding the characters—the actors of the catastrophe—in the anxiety and horror of a blinding present moment. As Northrop Frye observed in his *Fools of Time*, "the basis of the tragic vision is being in time, the sense of the one-directional quality of life, where everything happens once and for all, where every act brings unavoidable and fateful consequences, and where all experience vanishes, not simply into the past, but into nothingness, annihilation" (3). This sense of the present constantly moving forward feels like our everyday sense of how we live in this world: in David Kastan's words, "tragic time is, then, the experiential time of human life—a time, that like life itself to which it is inextricably tied, is directional, irreversible, and finite" (80).

Critics often contrast this sense of tragic time with that of comedy. For example, Matthew Wagner sees Shakespearean comedy as generating what he calls the "suspended time of the theater," a kind of "hetero-temporality" that is "separate from, but in dialogue with, the time of our everyday lives." In his thinking, this "suspended time is the forward motion of time [. . .] slowing or stopping altogether" (79). Wagner echoes here other critics' views that comedy generally takes place in a space—a tavern, country house, a forest—where clocks neither work nor matter. In tragedy, in contrast, it seems that the clock never stops: as Marlowe's Faustus knows in his final hour, no matter how much he cries out for more time, "The stars move still; time runs; the clock will strike" (A-Text 5.2.75).

This anxiety about tragic time also anticipates that both in a play and in our lives, all must come to an end. In establishing the meaning of being in time (or *Dasein*), Martin Heidegger came to focus on the end that is our death: "Only in dying," he wrote with profound pessimism, "can I to some extent say absolutely, 'I am'" (cited in Hoffman 222). When it comes to tragedy, as the Player in Tom Stoppard's *Rosencrantz and Guildenstern Are Dead* explains, it seems like the plot "never varies—we aim at the point where everyone who is marked for death dies" (79). We draw on Aristotle's painfully familiar words, that a tragedy must have a beginning, a middle, and most importantly, an end, both in a text and in performance. Classical tragedy ended with the exodus of the chorus, and Shakespeare's plays with a death march, an epilogue, or a song or jig. Now we know a play is over when the curtain closes or the house lights brighten. A tragedy must find its own way to an end, for characters, readers, and spectators alike.[1]

Yet while tragic performance may generate that feeling of a one-directional present, tragic temporality is surely more complicated than that, if only because the present is never solely present. In his *Conversations on Science, Culture, and Time* with Bruno Latour, Michel Serres posits that time is not linear, but rather it is "an extraordinarily complex mixture, as though it reflected stopping points, ruptures, deep wells, chimneys of thunderous acceleration, rendings, gaps—all sown at random or at least in a visible disorder" (57). For Serres, this is both theory of historical time and an assertion that every object is multitemporal, folding into itself many moments in time. Serres's thinking about time, linked to mathematical concepts of topology, was preceded by Edmund Husserl's as well as Heidegger's influential formulations of temporality. Husserl argued that we must reject the notion of time simply as "being," time as a sequence of moments of "now." Rather, in Robert Dostal's words in describing Husserl's thought, "we might say the present is 'thick' to the extent that, *within* the present, we find both the past and the future; that is, we find [there] all three dimensions of time [...]. [A]ny moment is what it is in virtue of what it retains of the past (retention) and what it anticipates of the future (protention)" (Dostal 125–6; see also Wagner chs. 1–2).

Tragedy thus could be said to generate for characters, readers, and audiences alike the anxiety of existing in the present, trembling between the awful certainty of the past and the unknown future. Yet that present is never fully and solely present. Rather, it is Husserl's "thick" present; it is Serres's folded time, in which the past erupts into the present, and we feel, as Lady Macbeth puts it, "the future in the instant" (1.5.66). Tragedy also brings its characters into collision with a temporality outside of everyday experience, the time of the gods or Providence, the divine beings that see past, present, and future simultaneously. Jean-Pierre Vernant has described how in Greek tragedy the audience experiences "a human, opaque time, made up of successive and limited present moments": this is the time which the audience understands as the present—as their present—in the enactment. Yet, he wrote, tragedy concurrently evokes the existence of "divine time" in which the confusion and contraction of human experience find their explanation and cause (19).

This chapter, and this book as a whole, will focus on how tragedy engages us in a sense of a present "thick" with past and future when it stages a crisis: a moment of decision in which everything changes. When Jacqueline de Romilly writes about Greek tragedy's being made possible by a new "consciousness of time" (5), she sees that "a short, continuous crisis, the origins and consequences of which cover a large span of time and distant connections [...] seems to be the double requirement of tragedy, and its double relationship to time" (12). That crisis of the moment requires a decisive action, action that may be informed by the past and determine the future, but which is experienced in the panic of the present. Once the action is taken, it appears that there can be no going back.[2] However, once we complicate the notion of tragic temporality, to see it as more multidirectional than merely linear, we can open up new ways of thinking about tragic causality and how choice operates in present time.

Positing that the present moment of decision may still be radically contingent, this chapter argues that in Greek and Shakespearean tragedy choice in a crisis can undermine as well as reinforce the kind of determinism that we conventionally associate with those plays. The first part of this chapter concerns the relationship between choice in time and dramatic character. A conventional view of tragedy assumes that a decision made in a moment of crisis springs from the hero's character, that is, choice is latent in his or her self, with its source a "tragic flaw." But I will consider how tragic character can be defined through choice, anticipating the deconstruction of character formation that will be explored in Chap. 4's discussion of videogames. In those anxious, blind moments of decision, the tragic characters become what they choose. This chapter's second part also questions the assumption that the tragic protagonist's choice might be equally constrained by the power that human beings have called the gods, fate, or destiny. While I declare here my bias in favor of free will, I do not aim to disentangle the paradoxes of fate and free will in tragedy once and for all in this short book. But I do take up the role of agency in the unfolding of events *in present time*: to what extent are we asked to imagine that the protagonist could act otherwise in a story that has already been written? As Frank Kermode has posed the task, we must then "concern ourselves with the conflict between the deterministic patterns any plot suggests, and the freedom of persons within that plot to choose and so to alter the structure, the relations of beginning, middle, and end" (*Sense* 30).

Such a short book also cannot responsibly consider the whole range of tragedy, and I make no claim to speak for all of it. Rather, I identify some examples where one could find the kind of openings to possibility that would lead a reader or actor to look for them elsewhere. So I will illustrate my points about the relationship of choice in time to character and consequences through a small set of plays: Aeschylus's *Oresteia*,

Sophocles's Theban plays, and Shakespeare's *Macbeth* and *Hamlet*. I have chosen these plays because my readers are likely to know them. Further, even when they are not being explicitly imitated, they continue to serve as powerful paradigms for the construction of tragic temporality and choice in time in many media.

CHOICE, CHARACTER, AND CONSEQUENCES IN GREEK TRAGEDY

Anyone who writes about tragedy, time, character, choice, and consequences must come to terms with Aristotle's *Poetics*, not because this "natural history" of tragedy is necessarily true, but rather because it has been so deeply influential. As a natural philosopher, Aristotle recognized that everything is constantly changing, like a tree that begins as a seed, grows tall, and dies (see Herman chap. 4). So too, when he lectured about plays, Aristotle observed that tragedy concerns the change in human lives over time. Tragedy enacts a structured version of that change, and, in Kathy Eden's words, holds out the hope that "fiction will disclose the causal connection between events and so deepen our understanding of those events—why they happened as they did" (45).

For Aristotle tragedy is "the mimesis not of persons (*anthropōn*) but of action and life (*praxēos kai biou*)," for "the events and the plot are the goal of tragedy." So, he says, "it is not in order to provide mimesis of character (*ēthē*) that the agents act; rather their characters are included for the sake of their actions" (*Poetics* 51). This formulation often confuses modern readers, who try to imagine plots without "characters"; plots do need people, for action, but what then is character? In defining *ēthos*, Aristotle wrote first that character is "that in virtue of which we ascribe certain qualities to the agents" (49); then he clarifies the point that "character is that which reveals a moral choice" (52–3). The *Poetics* thus connects character with choice, but what does Aristotle mean when he says that it "reveals" or clarifies choice? Edward Burns interprets the passage as saying that such moments of choice may indeed "show" the elements of a character (20), but "though we each possess a particular ethos, that is not for the Greeks the source of our defining reality; it is not 'ourself.' We are defined by the end to which our life tends, and that is achieved through our actions" (26). That is, the *Poetics* suggests that rather than characters being the wellspring of action, action and character function through mutual influence.

The relationship between character, choice, and action naturally entails questions of causality: if tragedy is about change, what precipitates it? How is that change connected to the idea that choice "reveals" character? The *Poetics* addresses these critical matters when discussing the tragic situations most likely to produce pity and fear. Aristotle specifies that the person experiencing a change of fortune should be "one who falls into adversity not through evil or depravity, but though some kind of error (*hamartia*)" (71). Many generations of commentators have struggled over the meaning of this statement, a controversy provoked by the fact that in Greek (in Halliwell's words) the word *hamartia* "embraces all the ways in which human vulnerability, at its extremes, exposes itself not through sheer arbitrary misfortune [. . .], but through erring involvement of tragic figures in their own sufferings" (17). Some read *hamartia* strictly as a simple "mistake" or an "error of judgment" enacted by what John Jones calls the "stage figure," who is as much as possible "like ourselves" (Jones, *On Aristotle* 39). For centuries, however, other critics have elevated the concept of Aristotle's "agent" or "stage figure" to the "tragic hero," and along with that translated *hamartia* as a "moral failing" or a "tragic flaw," the latent catalyst of that hero's downfall.

The distinction between an "error" and a "tragic flaw" is, of course, a crucial one. A mistake is something an agent *commits*; a tragic *flaw* is particular to a character that triggers effects or actions. Martha Nussbaum, for one, rejects the notion that Aristotle's *hamartia* means an inherent flaw, in concluding that "to come to grief through *hamartia*, then, is to fall through some sort of mistake in action that is causally intelligible, not simply fortuitous, done in some sense by oneself; and yet not the outgrowth of a settled defective disposition of character" (382–3). Her view contrasts with that of other critics accustomed to looking for that "tragic flaw" (often identified as *hubris* or pride) that precipitates a fall. So, for example, while struggling with Aristotle's authority, A.C. Bradley wanted to acknowledge the importance of "deeds" in Shakespearean tragedy, but those deeds, he wrote, must be "characteristic deeds": "What we do feel strongly, as a tragedy advances to its close, is that the calamities and catastrophe follow inevitably from the deeds of men, and that the main source of these deeds is character" (7). This is not time and place to decide what Aristotle meant by *hamartia*. Rather, I want to use the term's very ambiguity to complicate how we think about choice in a critical moment of time. Volumes have been written about the issue of moral choice and conflict in Greek tragedy, especially in the wake of Hegel's construction of ethical conflict as tragedy's essence. While obviously the social, philosophical, and political significance of the characters' moral choices matters immensely, my focus is more narrow: how choice with significant consequences is represented theatrically as happening *now*, in a constrained moment of present time.

The nature of time does influence both the characters' and the audience's experiences of these moments of decision. As I suggested as this chapter began, tragedy characteristically generates anxiety about time's passing, a precedent fully set by Greek tragedy, which, as Aristotle suggests, tends to enact action in time to make it seem as "real" as possible. The *Poetics* judges that the best tragedies represent a unified action within a short time span, at one point mentioning that their events tend to stay within a single revolution of the sun (47), a casual observation that later led to an obsession with rules governing the "unity of time." In performance, in particular, Greek tragedy's characteristic compression of events does make it seem as if a moment of decision happens almost in real time. In de Romilly's words, in such moments "the whole past and future will be mixed up in this special action: it is serious; it will decide; it is in the etymological meaning of the word, a 'crisis' (from *krinein*, meaning to 'judge' or to 'decide')" (10).[3]

While Aeschylus's *Oresteia* is both saturated with the past and full of foreboding for the future, each of the trilogy's plays stages a crisis of decision felt in this present of enactment.[4] Toward the beginning of *Agamemnon* a chorus recalls Agamemnon's past choice to sacrifice Iphigenia,[5] and later Clytemnestra's murder of Agamemnon serves as the play's climax. However, the critical choice *staged* here is *not* the queen's decision to murder her husband—that has been long planned—but rather Agamemnon's decision to walk on the elaborate tapestries that Clytemnestra spreads before the palace entrance. Treading on the tapestries means something and Agamemnon knows it, so he hesitates: he acknowledges that only the gods should walk on such glorious works, and just the idea of doing so fills him with fear. However, Clytemnestra persuades him to accede to her wish: "Oh, be persuaded," she says. "It is in your power, to heed me freely" (1. 943).[6] "Thus it is done," Agamemnon says, stepping on the tapestries, and entering into the palace, where he will be slaughtered (1. 950). While he thus responds to Clytemnestra's persuasion, Clytemnestra herself describes Agamemnon's choice as made freely. It is also consequential: it matters what he decides to do *here and now*, with the possibility that he might still refuse (especially since this is Aeschylus's plot invention). Yet, once done, his trampling the tapestries also symbolizes his life's record of transgression. As an act of hubris, it "reveals" his character and falls into place in the myth's chain of bloody acts, linked to the past and catalyzing the future. In this moment he becomes fully the Agamemnon whom Clytemnestra must destroy.[7]

In *The Libation Bearers*, the moment of present choice does concern murder, and thus even more clearly defines as much as it "reveals" character. The crisis comes when Orestes pauses in confronting his mother, when she asks if he has no feeling for her. Orestes then turns to his companion Pylades, asking "Pylades, what do I do? I am ashamed to kill my mother" (l. 899). Up to this point, the play presents an Orestes still unformed, and here for a moment it seems he could change his mind, even though we know that the story must play out. Pylades answers by reminding him of Apollo's oracles that directed him to revenge his father's murder. Orestes answers, "I judge that you win (*krinō se vikan*)" (l. 903). As de Romilly notes, the verb *krinō* is etymologically related to "crisis," thus linking his decision to this moment in time.[8] This moment of choice effects Orestes's transformation, turning him from a wavering young man into a matricide, just as Agamemnon's choice seals his death. At the same time, it represents Orestes's assent to the oracles, Apollo's words that embody the story as it must be told, and so Orestes's will then become one with the god's vision.

The *Oresteia*'s final play, *The Eumenides*, stages Orestes's trial for his mother's murder, where he is torn between the Furies's thirst for revenge and Apollo's force. Here the significant choice belongs not to a mortal but to a god. At the trial's climax, all anxiously await how Athena will cast her vote to determine Orestes's guilt. "It is left to me to judge (*loisthian krinai dikēn*)" (l. 734), she says, echoing Orestes's use of *krinō* in the preceding play. While up to this point she has represented herself as equally divided between Apollo's claims and the Furies's rage, here she casts her lot for Orestes because, she says, she is her father's child and must stand up for a father's rights. Here the "reveal" is of her identity, significantly aligned with a masculine ethos tying up the trilogy's gender dynamics.[9]

The *Oresteia* thus stages a complex interplay of choice, character, and consequences occurring in a moment of present crisis. Agamemnon's decision to tread on the tapestries is represented as a choice made in that moment that defines his arrogance and triggers his death, while it also functions to link past and future actions. Orestes is presented as on the cusp of becoming a character; his choice at the crisis, affirming the gods' oracles, makes him the full protagonist of his own story. *The Eumenides* then transforms the contingency of *mortal* choice by giving it to Athena, who confirms her identification with the masculine city she protects. The entire span of choice in the *Oresteia* moves from a small but resonant act in *Agamemnon* to a decision that has fundamental consequences for the future of Athens, when Athena announces the foundation of the Court of the Areopagus, which will judge crimes for generations of Athenians to come.

While the *Oresteia* thus stages significant moments of choice in time understood as both free and chained, Sophocles's Theban plays much more explicitly stage the tension between a personal, present choice and the temporality of prophecy.[10] I have written elsewhere about how prophecy in Greek tragedy distorts temporality, noting that oracles tend to be masterpieces of temporal indirection and thus confuse action in time: so, for example, when Oedipus asks about his parents and his past, he is answered by a statement of what he will do in the future (see Bushnell, *Prophesying*). The Theban plays exploit this weird openness of prophecy's temporality interacting with human agency. In *Antigone*, Tiresias seems to allow for events to turn out differently, if Creon changes his mind. In *Oedipus the King*, Apollo's oracles do not create that play's Oedipus who chooses to pursue the truth. And finally, the open nature of the conflicting prophecies in *Oedipus at Colonus* allows Oedipus to influence the future through his choices.

Antigone begins as *Agamemnon* does, when important decisions have already been made: Antigone has resolved to bury Polyneices, and Creon has announced he will punish anyone who does so. The action then plays out the consequences of either's *not* choosing otherwise, until the moment when Tiresias tries to get Creon to change his mind. Tiresias seems to offer Creon the possibility of averting a catastrophe: it is common, he says, for people to make mistakes or to commit a *hamartia*, and even once that mistake has been made, one can make amends (ll. 1024–27).[11] But Creon once again refuses, leading Tiresias to furiously prophesy Haemon's death. This prophecy ironically triggers Creon's panicked turn to the chorus for advice, as Orestes did to Pylades: "What must be done?" Creon cries (l. 1099). The chorus advises him to release Antigone, and he accedes, at this point recognizing that it is too hard to fight with necessity (l. 1106). Reversing the usual way that critical choice at once reveals and defines character, here choice breaks up Creon's character; the arrogant and stubborn king cracks and gives in. At the play's end, Creon confesses that he is now "no one" or "nothing" (l. 1325); his character has ironically been emptied out. In a further irony, we see that his choice is not timely and is thus inconsequential. It comes too late, unleashing the power of Tiresias's words that represent the story's end.

This Creon who cracks contrasts significantly with the Oedipus of *Oedipus the King*, who never changes his mind. One must always remember that the play itself does not portray the events of Oedipus's life. Rather, the *play*'s plot involves the hasty decisions Oedipus makes in responding to the oracle that the city must find who murdered Laius. In this play, in Bernard Knox's words, he is the image of a hero who is "not only free but fully responsible for the events that constitute the plot" (Knox, *Oedipus at Thebes* 12).[12] Each decision leads, step by step, to the play's crisis, Oedipus's interrogation of the old shepherd who knows the true story of Oedipus's birth. Even though Jocasta begs him to stop, Oedipus declares that he must not yield to her persuasion, and he hurtles forward. When the shepherd hesitates to speak, everyone's anxiety is acute. Even now it seems possible that it could all stop here, although Tiresias has obliquely threatened Oedipus with the riddle that "this day will give birth to you and destroy you" (l. 435). The herdsman says his next sentence is a terrible thing to speak, and Oedipus replies, so it is to hear: but it must be heard (*all'homōs akousteon*) (l. 1176).[13] Oedipus decides to push forward, choosing to know the truth, however dreadful, triggering the consequences of his own self-blinding and exile.

While the person exposed then is a parricide who has committed incest, Oedipus's act of choice reveals him as the man who seeks knowledge above all. David Orr argues that before he kills Laius at the crossroads, Oedipus is "neither a king nor a patricide, nor even a person he believes himself to be, since he's spent his life up to that point assuming he was the son of the wrong man. Before he makes the choice, he's nothing and anything. He is, you might say, pure potential" (166) (see also Sack 41). At this moment of choice in the play itself, Oedipus is at a very different kind of crossroads. Bernard Knox would argue that, as is the case with many of Sophocles's heroes, his decision "springs from the deepest layer of his individual nature" (Knox, *Heroic Temper*, 5), but this is also a moment that *defines* who Oedipus is.[14] At the same time that this act affirms Tiresias's prophecy generated in retaliation to Oedipus's assault, it is also an act of defiance that gives us an Oedipus who is neither tyrant nor criminal.

Oedipus's final act of choice in *Oedipus at Colonus* returns us to the radical contingency of prophecy evoked in *Antigone*. In this play a blind and aged Oedipus has come to the Eumenides's grove in Athens. Apollo has prophesied that he should find his rest there and bring blessings to his hosts and disaster to his enemies who exiled him from Thebes. The play's conflict arises from Creon's and Polyneices's efforts to bear Oedipus back to Thebes, for there Apollo has delivered new oracles that apparently place Thebes's future in Oedipus's hands if he dies there instead. The play thus sets up two possible outcomes in these two oracles which, as David Grene notes, makes Oedipus's story "an either-or chance, which may succeed or fail" (156).

Here Oedipus's choice *is* consequential for the future: Creon attempts to remove him by force, but Theseus defends him; Polyneices tries to move him by persuasion, but Oedipus only curses him. The play thus grants Oedipus himself a kind of prophetic power and control over his own future. By the play's end, when the thunder rumbles and the gods call on Oedipus to leave, Oedipus anxiously summons Theseus to share the secret of his resting place. Of all the moments in his life, Oedipus sees this as *his* crisis: in Robert Fagles's translation, he says to Theseus, "My life hangs in the balance" (*hropē biou moi*, l. 1508) (Sophocles, trans. Fagles, 374). But now his choice is to move where he was always going; he leaves freely, without help or support, led only by Hermes and Persephone, gods of the transition to the underworld.

I believe that if we thus focus on the tragic choices made in the present of enactment, all these plays thus offer a much more nuanced version of the interplay of tragic choice, character, and consequence than is commonly understood. Without a doubt, the plays' actions are bound up in the framework of stories or myths as they have always been told. Everything that happens in the *Oresteia* has its roots in the past and begets the future. At the same time, these plays themselves foreground the contingency of the protagonists' choices at a moment when they waver, when we are left to imagine "what if," until the foot falls, the heart hardens, or the vote is cast. Sophocles's plays further generate tension between granting meaning to the protagonist's choice and the necessity bound up in prophecy. The "pastness" of the story becomes modeled as the future, but within those stories the protagonists are given the opportunity to contest their limits. In contrasting Euripides's self-conscious tragedies with those of Sophocles and Aeschylus, Cedric Whitman asserts that "the two earlier poets foster the illusion that the mythic tale is creating or recreating itself" (114). But if that it is so, Sophocles and Aeschylus also allow their protagonists to participate in that mythmaking.

CHOICE, CHARACTER, AND CONSEQUENCES
IN SHAKESPEAREAN TRAGEDY

We might expect the dynamics of tragic time, choice, and consequences to work differently in Shakespearean tragedies, because ideas of both time and character must have changed so much in the long interim. Scholars commonly contrast Greek and neoclassical tragedy's constricted temporality with the temporal flexibility—even eccentricity—of most English Renaissance tragedy.[15] Further, audiences and scholars alike tend to grant Shakespeare's tragic characters a kind of depth and "inner life" that exceeds anything expected from Greek tragic protagonists. But surely Shakespearean tragedy is crisis-driven as well.[16] I want to ask the same question about Shakespearean tragedy that I did about the Greek plays: what happens to our assumptions about character and necessity if we focus on those recurrent crises, choices enacted in what feels like real time?

My case studies here will be *Macbeth* and *Hamlet*, both plays obsessed with time's passing and the protagonists' need to decide in a crisis. When Macbeth seizes the dagger to murder Duncan, *Macbeth* seals the construction of character through choice; in contrast, in *Hamlet*, where choice is consistently deferred, the protagonist's character remains in flux. Further, while the ambiguity of prophecy in *Macbeth* implies the multiple possibilities latent in the "seeds of time," only to have Macbeth close them down, *Hamlet* leaves open the possibility that plots or stories could be rewritten, under the play's conditions of profound uncertainty.

While certainly early modern English theatrical conventions mostly ignored classical models, Shakespeare does seem to have cared about time's passing both as a theme and as the condition of playing that defined tragic experience. While a few playwrights like Ben Jonson were interested in conforming to Aristotle's "unities," Philip Sidney was largely an outlier in condemning his contemporaries for their "liberality" regarding time (44–46). His ultimate referent was, of course, *The Poetics'* "single daylight period" allowed for tragic action. Most of Shakespeare's plays do resemble those that Sidney criticizes, covering the events of decades in "two hours space" (Sidney 45). Several do explicitly mark the present time of their staging: for example in *Henry V* the chorus announces that the audience is about to witness "th'accomplishment of many years / Into an hour glass" (Prologue 36–37); and in *The Winter's Tale* the chorus intrudes "in the name of Time, / To use my wings" and push events forward (5.1.3).[17]

These choric interventions in a history and a romance mark the poet's power, his presence in our present that mediates the past. But such figures rarely intervene in Shakespeare's tragedies. Instead, like their Greek predecessors, the tragedies seem to feed on the oppressiveness of the present time.[18]

As a history that is also a tragedy *Macbeth* is famously driven by a sense of great temporal urgency, compressing historical events that took place over more than a decade.[19] Actions press hard on one other in this play. No sooner have we heard the startling first prophecies from the Weird Sisters than Ross and Angus come to greet Macbeth as Thane of Cawdor. A hundred or so lines later, Lady Macbeth stands with Macbeth's letter in her hand, and Macbeth himself immediately arrives: as she declares, echoing what might be the audience's sentiments, "Thy letters have transported me beyond / This ignorant present, and I feel now / The future in the instant" (1.5.54–56).[20] The distinction between present and future blurs further as Macbeth's regicide spawns more murderous acts that do almost seem indeed to happen in an instant. When Malcolm asks in 4.3, "What's the newest grief?" Ross replies, "That of an hour's age doth hiss the speaker; / Each minute teems a new one" (4.3.175–6), evoking the audience's own experience of the playing time.

In the midst of this ongoing panic, Macbeth wants to master time. In first contemplating the terrible act of regicide, he speculates,

> If it were done when 'tis done, then 'twere well
> It were done quickly. If th'assassination
> Could trammel up the consequence, and catch
> With his surcease success: that but this blow
> Might be the be-all and the end-all, here,
> But here upon this bank and shoal of time,
> We'd jump the life to come. (1.7.1–7)

Here time, choice, and consequences run over each other. Macbeth fantasizes converting quick action, that moment when one usually feels out of control, into time stopped; with the moment repeated, then "done" and "done" would become the "be-all and the end-all." But his very words show one cannot stop the forward movement of time. The passage strains under the enjambment of the lines that fall forward, and "surcease" slips into "success," rather than repeating as the same word. The ironic consequence of Macbeth's regicide is that he does eventually feel trapped in a deadly present, a sequence of individual moments and days, as "tomorrow, and tomorrow, and tomorrow / Creeps in this petty pace from day to day / To the last syllable of recorded time." The play collapses into Macbeth's tragic day, his sequence of tomorrows that are equivalent to the time of playing or performance itself, when "Life's but a walking shadow, a poor player / That struts and frets his hour upon the stage, / And then is heard no more" (5.5.18–25).

Yet contradicting the tightening of Macbeth's time in this kind of present is the temporality of the Weird Sisters' prophecies. Collapsing so many categories (of the earth and not, women or not), the Weird Sisters seem to appear and disappear out of the play's time, as if "the earth hath bubbles" (1.3.77). While much of their prophecies' ambiguity is resolved by the play's end, their temporality is profoundly unstable. In Shakespeare's day, their final prophetic show of the eight kings would have connected the past to the present of *Macbeth*'s playing. In this climactic moment, the Weird Sisters answer the question that Macbeth's heart throbs to know: will "Banquo's issue ever / Reign in this kingdom?" (4.1.118–9). The answer comes in the procession of kings, the eighth with a "glass" that "shows me many more," some of whom carry the "two-fold balls and treble sceptres," referring to the Stuart royal line and King James who reigned when this play was first performed. The show is also the portal to an imagined future that lies beyond even that, stretching out to "th'crack of doom" (4.1.133). At the same time, the audience experiences their speaking of a future in an enacted present, while, as Marjorie Garber notes, for the playgoers in turn "the past becomes a future" ("What's Past," 306–7). Thus, the temporality of their prophecy runs simultaneously backward and forward.

In this layering in which time hurtles forward, oscillates, and bends, what then becomes of the critical choice in this play that Frank Kermode describes as Shakespeare's ultimate "play of crisis" (*Sense* 84)? Until the end of Act 1, Macbeth has not decided to kill Duncan: at the beginning of 1.7 he insists to Lady Macbeth that "we will proceed no further in this business" (l. 31). Only after some 50 lines of dialogue almost entirely taken up with his questions and his wife's answers does Macbeth declare, "I am settled, and bend up / Each corporal agent to this terrible feat" (ll. 79–80). He does not explain why he has changed his mind; it seems to just happen, while he is silent and Lady Macbeth speaks. Thereafter, in the soliloquy before the murder, we witness him summoning up those "corporal agents" to aid him in the murder, transforming the dagger of his mind into the dagger in his hand.

So what brings Macbeth to this decision, indirectly echoing Agamemnon's self-subjection to Clytemnestra? Recently Shakespeare scholars have vigorously debated how we should understand "character" in this period: as a product of ideology, the construction of personality through the passions and the "humors," or the kind of subjectivity we see as the mark of modernity.[21] My point here concerns *dramatic* character, where I would argue that this play, like the Greek tragedies I discussed above, ties action to the construction of character, which up to this point has been unfixed. Macbeth says, "To know my deed 'twere best not know myself" (2.2.71), but once he has committed the act of regicide, the deed becomes his self. Up to the point of Duncan's assassination, Macbeth is not stably defined as a character, when, as Lady Macbeth points out, he would and yet would not act, torn as to what sort of man he is. As Alan Sinfield describes it, up until that point the play has displayed his "radically insecure subjectivity, one swaying between divergent possible selves and vulnerable to manipulation" (64). But the assassination activates a chain of events, and Macbeth becomes his choice to kill, the murderer and tyrant whose acts emerge from that identity. In James Calderwood's words, "An act, as Macbeth knows even before he himself acts, is defined by its consequences, and a man may be defined by his acts. If Macbeth brings into being the act of regicide, that act reciprocates by bringing Macbeth into being in a new and murderous form" (343).

But if it is not a predefined character or "tragic flaw" that makes Macbeth a murderer, should we understand instead that the play's prophecies imply that such a choice was still predestined? Are prophecies like the dagger Macbeth sees that "marshal'st me the way that I was going" (2.1.42), that is, do the prophecies merely manifest Macbeth's desires, or do they indicate powers at work beyond himself? There are many reasons to doubt that the prophecies are fatal, the foremost being that all forms of soothsaying were very much under suspicion in Shakespeare's world (see Dobin). The Bible itself is filled with stories of false as well as true prophets, and in the Christian tradition prophecy was associated with the devil as well as God: so Banquo warns Macbeth that "oftentimes to win us to our harm / The instruments of darkness tell us truths, / Win us with honest trifles to betray's / In deepest consequence" (1.3.120–4). But any sense of the prophecies' fatality is also undermined by their unstable temporality. After the Weird Sisters have pronounced their "all hails" to Macbeth, Banquo asks these "imperfect speakers" if they "can look into the seeds of time / And say which grain will grow and which will not" (1.3.56–57). The image of the "seeds of time," some of which sprout and some which do not, suggests that the future is *not* fixed; rather, alternative stories are latent in that soil of existence. The play's nonlinear temporality opens up the possibility that events could be otherwise, before certain choices are made, before a decision that both fixes character and drives time inexorably forward.[22]

In many ways, *Macbeth* thus resembles its predecessor *Hamlet*: both are tragedies of time that stage a protagonist's agonized contemplation of action and the control of its consequences. However, whereas in *Macbeth* time presses relentlessly forward, in *Hamlet* time drags. Wylie Sypher has described *Hamlet*'s temporality as "punctiform time," where Hamlet's "life becomes a succession of agonizing instants, each a commencement deprived by the wonted context of the past" (66–7).[23] But the play's pace, with its dilated scenes, stops and starts, certainly contrasts with *Macbeth*'s urgent tempo. In what Claudius calls countless "abatements and delays" (4.7.118), *Hamlet* draws out and suspends the experience of present time.[24] In that context, it enacts multiple changes on the choice to act— or not—in time, asking what happens when you hesitate to act in a timely way; or when you act rashly and make a mistake; or when you choose not to choose, acknowledging instead a "divinity that shapes our ends" (5.2.10).

In the typical revenge tragedy (and Shakespeare is riffing on earlier revenge tragedies here), the protagonist does delay acting, but only because he is looking for just the right moment to achieve that revenge (and of course if he did not delay, it would be a very short play). In contrast, Hamlet seems to either miss the right moment (for example, failing to kill Claudius while he is praying) or just misfire, as when he stabs Polonius by mistake. James and Tita Baumlin have noted that thus "Shakespeare's ironic twist upon the typical revenge plot arises from his protagonist's *failure to act* in the 'right' moment" or the *kairos* (169). As Frank Kermode has put it simply, if *Hamlet* is in fact "a play of action," and Hamlet himself is "a player and an actor," "sometimes the play makes him a bad one" (*Riverside* 1189).

Where the choice to act is thus delayed or done in error, in what Kermode calls this play of "protracted crisis" or a suspended present (*Sense* 87), the construction of tragic character through choice is fundamentally disrupted. Hamlet's not killing Claudius while he is praying defers the question of what or who Hamlet is, and Hamlet himself cannot explain his own delay, as he confesses. "I do not know / Why yet I live to say, 'this thing's to do,' / Sith I have cause, and will, and strength, and means / To do't" (4.4 42–45). His mistaken killing of Polonius still leaves the question open: who is he? Does his rash stabbing of Polonius make him a murderer? Is that really "Hamlet" as he commits a murder that is both intentional and unintentional? Indeed, later Hamlet says to Laertes that it was not "Hamlet" who killed Polonius. Rather, it was Hamlet's madness: "Was't Hamlet wrong'd Laertes? Never Hamlet. / If Hamlet from himself be ta'en away, / And when he's not himself does wrong Laertes / Then Hamlet does it not; Hamlet denies it" (5.2.211–14). Hamlet himself thus separates himself, his "character," from that action, splitting open the idea of character itself and reducing it to a state of contingency.

What indeed do we do with the question of relating Hamlet's character to the play's action? In *Hamlet without Hamlet*, Margreta de Grazia details the astonishing two-hundred-year-old history of the question "Why Does Hamlet Delay," from the time when something like "psychology" first came into the picture (before then critics worried mostly about the play's plot). She notes how "answers to the question of Hamlet's delay keep piling up, from sensitivity, to excessive meditation, to melancholia, to guilt, to the wound of castration" (170). All of these readings do derive from the assumption, in A.C. Bradley's words, that "action is essentially the expression of character" (35).[25] If like de Grazia I resist the compulsion to pluck out the "heart of [Hamlet's] mystery" (3.2.357–8) and derive the play's action from his character, I am not saying that Shakespeare's culture did not allow for the idea of an "inner" self related to action. Both Hamlet and his observers worry about that "self." Claudius is concerned that "nor th'exterior nor the inward man / Resembles that it was," and he speculates Hamlet's father's death "hath put him / So much from th'understanding of himself" (2.2.5–10). In speaking to Horatio about Claudius's excessive drinking, Hamlet himself wonders whether it is because of habit or instead some "vicious mole of nature" that some men "shall in the general censure take corruption" (1.4.23–35): that is, he asks whether bad behavior is innate or learned.[26] My point here is simply that, in exploring the effects of choice deferred or disengaged from deliberation, *Hamlet* both foregrounds and questions the assumptions we make about the relationship between dramatic character and action: how does a play create a character out of a sequence of decisions and actions—and what happens when that process is continually deferred? One can see a productive as well as negative effect in such a delay: as Rayner observes of Hamlet's staying his hand, "To hold back means to keep possibilities open and to keep act and identity from becoming corpses" (107).

At the same time that the play thus challenges expectations about the relationship between dramatic character and timely choice, it also unsettles our assumptions about authorship and agency. Many readers of *Hamlet* have looked to Act 5 as the key to understanding the meaning of action in the play. There Hamlet tells Horatio of his actions on shipboard, where in acting "rashly" in the night, he sought out the commission Rosencrantz and Guildenstern were bearing to England. He associates this rashness, choosing without thinking, with a "divinity that shapes our ends, / Rough-hew them how we will" (5.2.10–11). At the same time, Hamlet's impulsive action leads to his rewriting the commission, thus creating what he sees as an alternative ending to his own story, sending Rosencrantz and Guildenstern to their deaths rather than himself. The play thus sends two potentially conflicting signals: a character can interfere in the "plot" or "plotting," yet that move itself is built into the play's overall scheme.

When faced by Osric's invitation to the fencing match with Laertes, Hamlet notoriously chooses not to choose, at the heart of "now." When he confesses to Horatio that he has a "gaingiving" about the match, Horatio urges him to "obey" that internal warning. Hamlet replies (in the Folio version): "Not a whit, we defie Augury; there's a speciall Prouidence in the fall of a sparrow. If it be now, 'tis not to come: if it bee not to come, it will bee now: if it be not now; yet it will come; the readinesse is all [. . .]" (Folio 280). Paradoxically, in the style of the tragic hero who defies the prophet, Hamlet thus resists the prophetic inkling of his own death by accepting that he will die eventually. These lines rehearse all possibilities of the relationship between "now" and the "time to come." But the pressure is on the "now," a word that is repeated three times in the Folio text, and on the verb "be": for this moment, he is inhabiting the present. In the Folio the last sentence of the speech reads further: "the readinesse is all, since no man ha's ought of what he leaues. What is't to leaue be-times?"; however, in the Quarto the lines are "The readines is all, since no man of ought he leaues, knowes what ist to leaue betimes. Let be" (as it is in Arden text, 5.2.197–201). The Quarto text (the preferred modern reading) does not refer to what a man has, but rather to the existential unknown: since we know nothing of "now," what difference does it make that we do not know the future? The last words of the Quarto text, "Let be," surely answer the question of "To be or not to be?" "Let be" transforms the anxiety of the present into acceptance of any possible future. The very instability of these lines among the three texts of *Hamlet* (the first quarto lacks them) underlines the contingency of any words about time. These words that speak of the future exist themselves in a state of uncertainty.

Eric Levy has observed that "Hamlet himself is intimately associated with hypothetical alternatives," with wishing and wondering and deferring, persisting in the "subjunctive mood" (167–8). Along with the act in which he rewrites Claudius's commission, the moment when Hamlet "defies augury" both opens up and closes off any possibilities that the story could end differently. There would, he imagines, be many alternative paths to the end, yet however, whenever, he says, "it will come" (5.2.199). This, of course, can be said to be the power of prophecy itself: in its riddling ambiguity, prophecy typically embeds multiple meanings. Different possibilities are in some sense always latent even if retrospectively the words seem to point to only one conclusion.

Wylie Sypher also reminds us that Hamlet's end comes in what should be an open-ended game, the fencing match with Laertes, a fiction of combat which turns out to be real combat (while it is also a part of a play) (86–89). Through *Hamlet*, Hamlet himself is the consummate player, the actor who mimes his own madness, who uses theater in cat and mouse game with Claudius, and who spars with his antagonists, whether verbally or physically. Joseph W. Meeker refers to this as "Hamlet's gamesmanship," where "Hamlet tries at every opportunity to convert actions into words, violence into argument, murder into games" (74–75). But what does this suggest of the play's "fatalism," if, as Roger Caillois has argued, we should understand all forms of play as activities that are essentially free and uncertain in their outcomes (9–10)? [27]

Hamlet's final confrontation with Laertes is a *game* that appears to be one of skill, matching two combatants, but it also is a murder *plot*, entailing Claudius's backup plan to poison Hamlet if the envenomed foil does not work. The structure of a *game* implies that within its rules, the outcome should be uncertain, depending on skill and chance. But this match is also a *plot* composed by Claudius and Laertes—and Shakespeare himself; open-ended gameplay thus collides with their narrative purpose. As Shankar Raman comments on the final combat, the result is that "No matter what the odds or initial expectations, the future refuses to be de-futurized, chance has its word" (202). While this catastrophe is often understood to reaffirm that "rashness" or "indiscretion" serves the ends of divinity when "our deep plots do fall" (5.2.9), the scene's rapidity and chaos reinforce the sense that for the moment, any outcome seems possible.

This is the moment to remember that in *Hamlet*'s source texts, Saxo Grammaticus and François de Belleforest's translation of it in *Histoires*

Tragiques, Hamlet does not die when he achieves his revenge: rather he violently severs his usurper uncle's head from his body, burns down the palace, and lives to reign as king. So it is entirely possible to think that Hamlet did not have to die at this play's conclusion, since that was *not*, in fact, the way that the story had always been told. Horatio's final report to Fortinbras emphasizes more the contingent nature of all the play's events, of all the "mischance" (5.2.378), "of carnal, bloody, and unnatural acts, / Of accidental judgements, casual slaughters. / Of deaths put on by cunning, and for no cause, / And in this upshot purposes mistook / Fall'n on th'inventors' heads" (5.2.365–9). The impression he leaves us with at the end is less the image of that "special providence in the fall of a sparrow" and more of an open world of force and accident, cunning and casual slaughter.

This view of *Hamlet* as a form of gaming draws our attention to the way in which both character and plot in the play can be seen as unfixed and contingent, played out in a suspended present time, while at the same time the notions of plotting and "providence" are operational. In writing about all sorts of games, Greg Costikyan reminds us that "part of the reason games appeal to us is because they allow us to explore uncertainty, a fundamental problem we grapple with every day, in a non-threatening way" (location 218). Critics of tragedy usually emphasize the opposite point, focusing on how tragedy eliminates uncertainty by constructing a shape that connects events and clarifies causality in retrospection. However, if we look instead for the ways in which the structures of gaming underlie tragedy, another image emerges of a more dynamic tension between action and consequences played out in the present. Remembering Hamlet's "gamesmanship" sets a direction for the next three chapters of this book, which explore the transformation of tragic paradigms of choice in present time in adaptation and performance, time-travel films, and videogames, which restore the environment of uncertainty to time and offer the invitation to play.

NOTES

1. For an important meditation on tragic structure and endings, see Kermode 2000. See also Snyder, Chap. 1 and Wagner, Chap. 2.
2. See also Kirkland, who comes at the issue from the point of fate/free will (Kirkland 2014).
3. Also see Kermode, who follows how, through our fictions, we draw out of *chronos*, the undifferentiated stream of time, the *kairos* or the crisis; then the

chronos time that is "simply successive becomes charged with past and future" (45). So, he observes, "the moments we call crises are both ends and beginnings" (96) (Kermode 2000).

4. See de Romilly: "Each action is made to bear on the whole history of the house of Atreus; the weight of the past is felt as heavier, the anxiety as more devastating, the issue as of more meaning" (13) (de Romilly 1968). See also Widzisz for a valuable summary of the work to date on temporality in the *Oresteia* (Widzisz 2012).

5. See Nussbaum on Agamemnon's decision to sacrifice Iphigenia as it is represented in the chorus at the play's beginning: "Agamemnon is allowed to choose: that is to say, he knows what he is doing [...] nothing forces him to choose one course rather than another. But he is under necessity in that those alternatives include no very desirable options" (34) (Nussbaum 2001).

6. Citations are from Aeschylus, *Septem Quae Super Sunt*; translations are my own (Aeschylus 1972).

7. See Widzisz on how here "Agamemnon finds himself suddenly at the cross-currents of two identity shifts" (57) (Widzisz 2012).

8. Compare Jean-Paul Sartre's adaptation of this moment in *The Flies*, where the decision is seen as coming as a *coup de foudre*: "Suddenly, out of the blue, freedom crashed down on me and swept me off my feet[...] And there was nothing left in heaven, no right or wrong, or anyone to give me orders" (118) (Sartre 1989).

9. For an important account of the gender dynamics of *The Oresteia*, see Zeitlin, "Dynamics" (Zeitlin 1978).

10. See Hutchinson on the "aspect" of time in Sophocles (Hutchinson 1999).

11. Citations are from Sophocles, *Fabulae*; translations are my own unless indicated otherwise (Sophocles 1975).

12. See also Segal, *Oedipus Tyrannus*: "He is both free and determined, both able to choose and helpless in the face of choices that he has already made in the past or circumstances (like those of his birth) over which he has no power of choice" (76) (Segal 1993).

13. The Greek is ambiguous here, in implying compulsion, but without designating the source of the compulsion.

14. See Segal, *Oedipus Tyrannus*: "Oedipus does *not* have a tragic flaw [...]. Oedipus's haste and irascibility at crucial moments [...] contribute to the calamity but are not sufficient reasons for it nor its main cause" (76) (Segal 1993).

15. See Bushnell, "Time and History," for a short summary of the adaptation of the unities in England in the sixteenth century (Bushnell 1990). In an article on Shakespeare's disdain for the unities, Ernest Schanzer describes Prospero's self-harassment in the observation of time as the playwright's "last thrust in his

scattered skirmishes against that bloated, tyrannical upstart, the doctrine of the unity of time" (61) (Schanzer 1975).

16. Kermode has observed of Shakespearean tragedy, "It offers imagery of crisis, of futures equivocally offered, by prediction and by action, as actualities; as a confrontation of human time with other orders, and the disastrous attempt to impose limited designs upon the time of the world" (88) (Kermode 2000).

17. Unless otherwise indicated, quotations are from *The Riverside Shakespeare* (1974).

18. For more extensive consideration of time in Shakespearean tragedy see Kastan (1982), Wagner (2014), Waller (1976), and Sypher (1976).

19. There has been a vast amount of scholarship on time in *Macbeth*, and my own observations just scratch the surface: for the most recent articles, which also provide references to earlier scholarship, see Macdonald (2010) and Marchitello (2013). See also Rayner, Chap. 3 (Rayner 1994).

20. All citations from *Macbeth* are from *The Norton Shakespeare: Tragedies* (1997).

21. See Sinfield's discussion of character criticism and the post-structuralist critique (Sinfield 1992). See Yachnin and Slights for a counterargument for the function of "character" as a "valid analytic category" (3) with a focus on theater and performance, and where an interest in character trumps plot (7) (Yachnin and Slights 2008). See also Mazer on the issues related to character and performance (Mazer 2015).

22. See Rayner, on the Weird Sister as figures of the potentiality of the verb "do" without an object, where "I'll do" is "both obdurately closed to negotiation and indefinitely open" (61) (Rayner 1994).

23. See also Everett: "the play leads us unusually often to think of it in terms of the laws of time, and to call *Hamlet*, if we wish, a Time Play" (119); she says of Hamlet that he is "always potential and always too late" (123) (Everett 1977).

24. All quotations from *Hamlet* are from the Arden edition, ed. Thompson and Taylor (2016).

25. Compare Barker on Hamlet: "At the centre of Hamlet, in the interior of his mystery, there is, in short, nothing" (37) (Barker 1995).

26. Reacting against the new historicist and cultural materialist image of the early modern socially constructed self, Katherine Maus has usefully focused on this period's obsession with differentiating the "private" and "public" self (Maus 1995).

27. See Rayner on how we might think of fatality in *Hamlet* as "the limits of the game in which rules constrain action but do not dictate how the game is played out. That is left to a combination of chance and skill: [...] Plot is the evidence of the fatality of the game" (119–120) (Rayner 1994). See also Costikyan on the conditions of openness and uncertainty in games (Costikyan 2013).

CHAPTER 2

Tragic Adaptation and Performance: Undoing the Play

Abstract This chapter investigates how through dramatizing choice in "real" time, both adaptation and performance can release alternative stories or endings in a tragic play. Audiences and directors certainly debate how far may one go in "correcting" or making changes in a tragic plot, since tragedy seems to be all about fatal consequences and especially an ending from which there is no return. Radical remakings of tragic plots through either adaptation or performance are admittedly rare, precisely because audiences, actors, and critics alike often crave the repetition of those familiar stories, no matter how horrific they might be. However, this chapter offers two case studies of performative disruption that help us see the alternative possibilities latent in tragic theater. The first example is Tom Stoppard's *Rosencrantz and Guildenstern Are Dead*, an adaptation of both *Hamlet* and Samuel Beckett's *Waiting for Godot*. *Rosencrantz and Guildenstern* stages the dynamics of choice in an unfixed present time and space to exploit the opening for invention, gaming, and rewriting that *Hamlet* itself invites. In the end Stoppard does not let Rosencrantz and Guildenstern escape from *Hamlet*; that is, he does not release the kind of potential that was exploded in this chapter's second example, Richard Schechner's legendary adaptation and performance of Euripides's *Bacchae* in *Dionysus in 69*. In that case, game-like performance generated a sense of present possibilities that could empower the audience and actors to intervene in the tragic plot and break it open—or to just walk away.

R. Bushnell, *Tragic Time in Drama, Film, and Videogames*,
DOI 10.1057/978-1-137-58526-4_2

Keywords Performance · Adaptation · Theater · Play · Games · Fate · Choice · Crisis · Tragedy · Drama · Time · Audience · Temporality · Richard Schechner · Participatory theater · Tom Stoppard · *Rosencrantz and Guildenstern Are Dead* · *Dionysus in 69* · Samuel Beckett · *Waiting for Godot* · The Performance Group · Shakespeare · *Hamlet*

When choosing to act, the protagonists of classical and English Renaissance tragedy are bound up precariously in a diegetic present that links past and future yet is also open to the possibilities and even play that live performance enhances and complicates. As Stanley Cavell observes, tragic performance seems to demand "a continuous attention to what is happening at each here and now, as if everything of significance is happening at this moment, while each thing that happens turns a leaf of time" (93). But the audience is also inhabiting another kind of "now": in Thomas Whitaker's words, the spectators "are both 'outside' and 'inside' its action, in a double 'now' that is a mimed present and a present miming" (*Fields of Play* 16).[1] However much we feel that in watching a play we enter another kind of time and space, we know we are still sitting in our seats, passing a few hours of our own lives that touch on but are distinct from the play's time: in Richard Schechner's words, we do "a specific 'there and then' in this particular 'here and now' in such a way that all four dimensions are kept in play" (*Performance Theory* xiv). It is a strange experience: while we accept the suspension of ordinary time when the play begins, we still inhabit it, breathing, fidgeting, or hearing our seatmate's little noises.

How do we then experience those different "theres" and "thens"? In the theater past time may be signaled through sets or costumes: the Elizabethan ruff and doublet, or the cluttered furniture of the nineteenth-century drawing room.[2] "Original Practices" performances of early modern theater may also seek to recreate the past through acting and staging,[3] offering the heady sense of the past produced materially in the present. But audiences are always observing such plays from their own "future," and when the spectators know the story or script in advance, even when the play begins they await the end, watching for what they believe they know what will come. As Matthew Wagner has argued, while theater may appear to lock us in the present moment, a performance is powerful in "its marked constitution of past and future, its trumpeting of its beginning and end not as they line up sequentially, but as they stack simultaneously" (32). Like prophecy, performance is always looking both backward and forward, even while it engages us in the present.

The temporality of performance matters when it comes to choice because in performance, actions and choice happen in an environment full of contingency, reflecting the uncertainty I have suggested is already latent in the tragic plot. As spectators, the more that we feel that there is a plan, the more we attend to the deviations, however slight. Even when a script has been established, every performance represents an intervention, whether by actors, directors, or producers. During a performance, actors and audience together create and witness an event in a present time ripe with potential. When both audience and actors might be recalling a "script," a sense of risk always haunts a live performance. We know intuitively that anything could happen: a fall on stage, a moment of brilliant improvisation, or a spectator's heart attack, and every performance differs, however slightly, from the next.[4]

In the case of classical and early modern tragedy, performance also embodies the uncertainty embedded in the script itself. Scholars now always remind us of the instability of the texts of premodern plays; because of the vagaries of textual transmission, very few of these play texts can be said to be authoritative or even authorial. In discussing *Hamlet*'s openness to change, I have already pointed to its radical textual variability. Composing any printed text of *Hamlet* involves a dizzying array of editorial choices, some of them apparently trivial and others more consequential,[5] which are then also open for selection by actors and directors. William Worthen thus sees that this "fungibility of the theatrical text" inherent in early plays "is preserved in the scandalous notion that actors and directors intentionally alter the text, marking it up with their highlighters, cutting passages, moving some and adding others, changing individual speeches to make them more comprehensible or inoffensive, and—especially in the case of stage directions—ignoring some words altogether" (*Force* 53).[6]

This chapter investigates how, through dramatizing choice in what feels like real time, both adaptation and performance might release alternative stories or endings in a tragic play. When it comes to a known story, audiences and directors certainly differ on how much interference of this kind they can tolerate. Especially in the case of tragedy, they debate how far one may go in "correcting" or making changes, since tragedy seems to be all about fatal consequences and especially an ending from which there is no return. Radical remakings of tragic plots through either adaptation or performance are admittedly rare, precisely because audiences, actors, and critics alike often crave the repetition of those familiar stories, no matter how horrific they might be: what Bertholt Brecht calls "barbaric delights" (189) or Philip Sidney "sweet violence" (28). However, here I offer two case studies of performative disruption that do help us see the possibilities latent in tragic theater. My first example is Tom Stoppard's *Rosencrantz and Guildenstern Are Dead*, an adaptation of both *Hamlet* and Samuel Beckett's *Waiting for Godot*. *Rosencrantz and Guildenstern* stages the dynamics of choice in an unfixed present time and space to exploit the opening for invention and rewriting that *Hamlet* itself invites. In the end Stoppard does not let Rosencrantz and Guildenstern escape from *Hamlet*; that is, he does not release the kind of potential that was exploded in my second example, Richard Schechner's legendary adaptation and performance of Euripides's *Bacchae* in *Dionysus in 69*. In that case, performance generated a sense of present possibilities that could empower the audience and actors to intervene in the tragic plot and break it open—or to just walk away.

Linda Hutcheon asks us to recognize that "by their very existence, adaptations remind us there is no such thing as an autonomous text or an original genius that can transcend history, either public or private. They also affirm that this fact is not to be lamented" (111). Theater scholars typically think of "adaptation" as the modern retelling or "remediation" of earlier plays. But of course, from the very beginning Greek tragedies were adaptations themselves, drawing on a common storehouse of myth and stories. Most often the plays stuck to the known general shape of the mythic plots, but they also could significantly alter them, as, for example, Euripides did in his *Helen*, which draws on Herodotus's speculation that Helen never actually went to Troy. So Alan Sommerstein concludes that "Tragedians never felt in the least inhibited about presenting or presupposing different and incompatible versions of a story in different works" (168). Renaissance tragic dramatists also freely changed their sources, whether histories or fictions, in order to create new plots. Shakespeare himself was a master adapter, most notoriously converting a story about King Lear that ended well in his source texts into the devastating end that he produced with Lear's and Cordelia's deaths. Modern playwrights, screenplay writers, and directors struggle much more with how they are bound to the narrative they are using, wondering at what point, when altered, the story becomes something else entirely.[7]

Adaptations are thus pulled between the poles of what Julie Sanders calls "dependence and liberation" (6). The critical discourse concerning adaptation usually bristles with a vocabulary of both power and emotion, summed up in the idea of "fidelity," the notion that we judge an adaptation by its faithfulness to a source text. All of these terms imply considerable anxiety about authorial freedom and agency. In exploring the "ethics of infidelity" in adaptation studies, Thomas Leitch notes how this language of fidelity signals concern about authority and obedience: he cites as an example the Hollywood producer David O. Selznick's criticism of filmmakers who deviate from their sources as those who "insist upon throwing away something of proven appeal to substitute things of their own creation" and thus asserting their own egos. Leitch sees Selznick as convicting such adapters of "a sin of hubris, a usurpation not so much of the author's function as of the author's prerogatives, committed by film-makers who mistakenly think themselves authors" (64). Leitch's own language suggests a resemblance between the tragic hero's "hubristic" resistance to prophecy and adaptation's defiance of its "source." For Leitch, in this sense, "infidelity" becomes a positive and even a kind of political act, "as a response to an injunction to be fruitful and multiply untrammeled by repressive social laws and mores" (66). Such attitudes also prevail in accounts of postcolonial adaptations of Western plays: for example, Helen Gilbert and Joanne Tompkins maintain that "rewriting the characters, the narrative, the context, and/or the genre of the canonical script provides another means of interrogating the cultural legacy of imperialism" (16).[8]

Although critics can thus variously configure adaptation as betrayal or resistance, it can also be construed as a constructive relationship. In writing about transmedial adaptations of Shakespeare, Diana Henderson uses the term "diachronic collaboration" to describe how adaptation can focus "attention on the connections among individuals, allowing artists credit and responsibility, but at the same time refusing to separate them from their social location and the work of others" (8; see also Rozett). Rather than just being seen as implicitly hostile or merely supplementary, adaptation looks more like a productive interaction. For example, in a study of *Moby-Dick* as adapting Shakespearean tragedy, John Bryant describes Melville as not just "liberated" from Shakespeare but also "liberating" Shakespeare, insofar as in *Moby-Dick* Melville "frees Shakespeare to speak what previously was unspoken or even unspeakable" (53). As is the case for Leitch, Bryant's language here is explicitly political, if in a more liberal democratic vein: "Adaptation is not only inevitable; it is a form of retelling that is so inherently irresistible to human beings that it is an inalienable right. [...] In this regard, adaptation may be seen as an epitome of multicultural democracy with its inescapable anxieties over the evolution of one's ethnicity, the threats of assimilation, the forging of a new identity and the retention or forgetting of past identities" (55). In such a formulation, adaptation still involves contesting the authority embodied in primary authorship, but it goes beyond critique to find an opening in the source itself, freeing voices and possibilities that were always already there.[9]

GAMING HAMLET: *ROSENCRANTZ* *AND GUILDENSTERN ARE DEAD*

Shakespeare's *Hamlet* itself functions as an adaptation of a narrative found in the *Historica Danica* of Saxo Grammaticus and then rewritten by François de Belleforest in his *Histoires Tragiques*, which scholars believe was in turn the source for the lost so-called *Ur-Hamlet*. The history of *Hamlet* is thus all about altering the story—and for Shakespeare, it also meant changing the end. At the end of Chap. 1, I argued that in his *Hamlet*, Shakespeare entertained the possibility that the story could be told anew, when Hamlet recounts his own history of rewriting Claudius's plot, resulting in the deaths of Rosencrantz and Guildenstern instead of his own. Hamlet himself is a radical adapter of plots and plays: he changes *The Murder of Gonzago* by inserting his own speech, a play of which he tells us "the story is extant, and written in very choice Italian" (3.2.255–6). While Hamlet suggests that all the acts of rewriting could be swept up in that force called the divinity that shapes our ends, the end still does not feel like fate when it is set in the structure of a game, which is both open-ended and overdetermined.

Into this play, in turn, stepped Tom Stoppard, the pirate playwright who forced open the plot fissures buried in the roles of two minor characters in order to make a play of his own. *Rosencrantz and Guildenstern Are Dead* brilliantly parodies its Shakespearean source while it also explores the question of how tragic plots are made and how characters and stories are fashioned in the present of playing.[10] In response to Rosencrantz's query, "what is your line?" the Player responds: "Tragedy, sir. Deaths and disclosures, universal and particular, denouements both unexpected and inexorable, transvestite melodrama on all levels including the suggestive." And, he reminds us, "It costs little to watch, and little more if you happen to get caught up in the action, if that's your taste and times being what they are" (23). While the Player thus apparently invites Rosencrantz and Guildenstern to have sex with his actors, he is also challenging them to cross the line from watching to cocreating a tragedy. How can they find their way into the story and become adapters in this play so fundamentally concerned with the problem of acting and action itself?

But *Hamlet* is not the only play *Rosencrantz and Guildenstern* adapts. As has been widely acknowledged, the play also owes an immense debt to *Waiting for Godot*, Samuel Beckett's own "tragicomedy" of inaction and delay. *Rosencrantz and Guildenstern* brings *Hamlet* and *Godot* together to give us characters confronted with the consequences of choosing to act—or not—in time. As in *Hamlet* and *Godot*, *Rosencrantz and Guildenstern* frames the problem of action in terms of notions of playing: play understood as tragic and comic theater and play as games. All three dramas reflect on how plays and games structure human experience where temporality, chance, and agency interact.[11]

For *Rosencrantz and Guildenstern*'s reader, the opening stage direction sets the tone for the play's postmodern temporality: "Two Elizabethans passing the time in a place without any visible character" (11). This setting strikes a vivid contrast with *Hamlet*'s beginning: there, the fourth and fifth lines are Francisco's comment to Barnardo, "you come most carefully upon your hour" and Barnardo's reply that "Tis now struck twelve," signaling this play's persistent concern with time's passage, whether events happen too soon (the marriage) or too late (the revenge). The *Rosencrantz and Guildenstern* stage direction appears to mark "then and there" by introducing two "Elizabethans," appropriately costumed, we assume. But the place itself has "no character," and what they are doing is "passing time" in the present by playing a coin-toss game. As the stage direction indicates further, "they have apparently been doing this for some time."

Much of Rosencrantz and Guildenstern's opening conversation concerns the puzzle of the game in which that coin keeps on coming up heads. They consider this as a temporal conundrum, because probability, like prophecy, is a time-bound phenomenon, involving the relationship between past, present, and future when an action is repeated. So they speculate that either the coin is always coming up heads because "time has stopped" or because each moment is isolated from the previous and subsequent one (if we consider each throw of the coin as separate from each other, there is always a 50–50 chance of its coming up heads) (16). In any case, Rosencrantz and Guildenstern really do not know what time it is: they fear they are too late, but they do not know for what. Throughout the play they speculate about the time of day by tracking the appearance of light, but they are constantly confused as to the light's direction; disorientation in space thus muddles time.

The theatrically experienced spectator will soon recognize that here Stoppard has summoned up the characters, action, and framework of *Waiting for Godot*, which itself begins with simple spatiotemporal coordinates: "A country road. A tree. Evening" (1). In his "tragicomedy in two acts" Beckett ironically adheres to the neoclassical rules of dramatic representation, whereby the stage should represent just one time and one place, so that the passage of time represented matches as closely as possible its present duration in performance. As Jean Chapelain put it in a letter to Pierre Godeau in 1630, it was neoclassical doctrine that "imitation in all works of art must be so perfect that no difference appears between the thing imitated and the thing that is imitating it, for the main source of effectiveness for the representation is to proffer objects to the mind as if they were true and present" (cited in Goodkin, 384). That is, the audience should live through the course of events being enacted before them just as they experience sitting in the theater, in the present and in their presence. For Vladimir and Estragon, that time stretches between one evening in Act 1 to the next day: "Same time, same place" (61), broken only by an imagined night which is also the audience's interval or intermission.[12]

While *Rosencrantz and Guildenstern* and *Godot* both unfold in the same unmarked, suspended present that the audience experiences, *Godot* sets the precedent that we should actually worry about just "passing time." While Estragon seems more indifferent,[13] over the course of the play Vladimir is increasingly desperate to locate them temporally. Not only does Vladimir feel he needs to know the day of the week, so they can keep their appointment (7), but more intuitively he seems to recognize that time matters, because time grounds memory, history, causality, and consciousness itself. The urgency of temporality surfaces most vividly in Pozzo's eruption in Act 2 responding to Vladimir's insistent asking him "when": when did Pozzo become blind and Lucky dumb, Vladimir wants to know, "Since when?" To this question Pozzo replies furiously, "Have you not done tormenting me with your accursed time! It's abominable! When! When! One day, is that not enough for you, one day he went dumb, one day I went blind, one day we'll go deaf, one day we were born, one day we shall die, the same day, the same second, is that enough for you?" (103). This is a different Pozzo from that of Act 1, who carries his half-hunter watch (until he loses it) and worries about his schedule. In Act 2, Pozzo has lost his sense of time along with his sight, and with it, any thought that time matters. His dismissal of time also reveals his profound moral void: if one cannot answer "when," one cannot answer "why," and so causality and responsibility do not matter, because logically nothing precedes an event.[14] Vladimir, in contrast, wants to know "when," because he senses that time is linked to consequences, connecting acts of the past, present, and future: "Tomorrow," he ponders, "when I wake, or think I do, what shall I say of to-day?" (104). He implicitly connects this "today," which will have become the past, to something that should have been done, a choice to be made "while the others suffered" (81). The play's concern with how we are "tied" or bound to one another (with Vladimir's and Estragon's asking how they are "tied" to Godot [16–17] and Pozzo and Lucky literally linked by a rope) thus stretches over time as well as space.

The shape of time and causality also serves to define two kinds of dramatic genres embedded in *Waiting for Godot*. While, as I have suggested, *Godot* generates the paralyzing present of neoclassical tragedy, it is also a *tragicomedy* with two intersecting plots, one of Vladimir and Estragon and the other of Pozzo and Lucky, each with a distinct pattern of action over time. Vladimir and Estragon's pattern involves repetition and routines, in the episodic style of vaudeville or gameplaying (later echoed in *Rosencrantz and Guildenstern*'s repeated coin tosses or their game of questions). While the most obvious analogy is thus old-style comedy, Bert States describes this effect as the temporality of history, which opposes the tragic plot of Pozzo and Lucky, with their exemplary reversal of fortune or "tragic fall" that is realized in all the characters' literal falling down in Act 2. In States's formulation, "tragedy (the isolation and death of the hero) completes its action, implying that everything that is important happens at one fatal time; the history play (the trials of the nation, or a race) implies a fresh beginning in every ending [...] and assures us that what has been done will have to be done again and again" (85). That is, from this perspective tragic time appears to close down all options, while both comedy and history have to allow for variation and renewal. In which framework, then, are we to see action in time: do we make a choice that changes everything, or is life simply a matter of repetition, time and again?

While *Godot* thus provides the model for *Rosencrantz and Guildenstern*'s two characters unmoored in space and "passing time" by talking and playing games, more importantly it constructs a game-like framework for asking these urgent questions about causality and responsibility implied in acting in time.[15] So Rosencrantz and Guildenstern's game of the coin toss means more than just how time is "passed." The phenomenon that the coin somehow, improbably but quite possibly, always ends up as heads, leads to the questions of "how" and "why," for which there are several possible answers. In differentiating such games of chance as the coin toss from games of contest that entail skill, Roger Caillois presents the common view that the game of chance "signifies and reveals the favor of destiny. The player is entirely passive; he does not deploy his resources, skill, muscles, or intelligence. All he need do is await, in hope and trembling, the cast of the die" (17). However, if each toss of the coin is to be considered as a single toss, in a repeated present moment, the only answer to "why" may indeed be simply "chance": in Greg Costikyan's words, "in a civilization based on scientific rationalism, we know that randomness is just randomness" (location 1273), and after all a coin toss is really a "stochastic system," and "in a stochastic system, each event is unrelated to the previous one" (location 1286). Rosencrantz and Guildenstern are understandably curious to know whether they are operating "within un-, sub- or supernatural forces" (17), and one should not consider the matter settled. As Guildenstern says, when they begin interacting with Hamlet, everything that is about to happen is a "game" anyway (40), and as I have suggested above, uncertainty and openness should be critical features of games.[16]

When the tragedians enter offering the pleasure of playing tragedy (which Rosencrantz later calls a "game"—"all filth" [29]), Rosencrantz tosses the coin again. In that context, the coin game, the tragedians' practice, and the play itself are all subject to the same question of "how" or "why," beginning with how the players came to be here, whether by chance or fate:

> *Guil:*   It was chance, then?
> *Player:* Chance?
> *Guil:*   You found us.
> *Player:* Oh yes.
> *Guil:*   You were looking?
> *Player:* Oh no.
> *Guil:*   Chance then.
> *Player:* Or fate.
> *Guil:*   Yours or ours?
> *Player:* It could hardly be one without the other.
> *Guil:*   Fate then.
> *Player:* Oh yes. We have no control. Tonight we play to the court. Or the night after. Or to the tavern. Or not. (25)

While first he attributes their meeting to chance, the Player thus appears finally to confirm that they are all acting out a story that has already been written, like the "tragedies of antiquity," those "great homicidal classics" (32). This definition of tragedy entails a "design" in which "events must play themselves out to the aesthetic, moral and logical conclusion," a conclusion where "everyone who is marked for death dies" (79). When Guildenstern asks *who* decides, the Player sidesteps the question, moving from the active to the passive tense: "*Decides?* It is *written.*" He thus avoids the question of agency, merely saying that all that they do as "tragedians" is "follow directions—there is no *choice* involved. The bad end unhappily, the good unluckily. That is what tragedy means" (80). This flip answer echoes Pozzo's view of events, in which it does not make sense to ask "when" and thus "why," if there is no choice involved, and when, in any case, we are all born to die: in Pozzo's words, "They give birth astride of a grave, the light gleams an instant, then it is night once more" (103).

But who is to say that the Player is an authority on the matter of the play? *Rosencrantz and Guildenstern*'s complex interplay of agency, choice, and writing, embodied in Stoppard's own rewriting of *Hamlet*, surely undermines such a conventional view of tragedy as "what is written." In Act 3 Stoppard offers another model for the play itself as a game, when Rosencrantz and Guildenstern describe "life on a boat" (116). When on the boat heading to England, they discuss whether they can speak to Hamlet, and both cheerfully acknowledge that it is "allowed":

> *Guil:* [...] We are not restricted. No boundaries have been defined, no inhibitions imposed. We have, for the while, secured, or blundered into, our release, for the while. Spontaneity and whim are the order of the day. Other wheels are turning but they are not our concerns. We can breathe, we can relax. We can do what we like and say what we like to whomever we like, without restriction.
>
> *Ros:* Within limits, of course.
>
> *Guil:* Certainly within limits. (116)

While Guildenstern's celebration of their freedom is thus undercut, and while they do think in the end that they made a mistake getting on a boat (122), as William Gruber has argued it is in this final act of the play where they could be seen as most free, precisely because this action is not scripted in *Hamlet* itself. The action here "exists between the lines, as it were, of *Hamlet,* in what has always been represented as an undefined, unwritten zone. Stoppard here invites his characters to invent their history according to their will. He offers them alternatives, if not absolute choice" (304–5).

In this distinct window of present time and action not enacted in *Hamlet,* playing the game and literally "at sea," Rosencrantz and Guildenstern confront the critical choice of what to do once they discover that the letter they bear condemns Hamlet to death. Rosencrantz raises the question obliquely as to whether they should transmit this text and death sentence: "We're his *friends*," he says, in apparent protest. Guildenstern responds passively, echoing the Player's (and Pozzo's) fatalism: all men must die someday, he says, and in any case "we are little men, we don't know the ins and out of the matter, there are wheels within wheels, etcetera—it would be presumptuous of us to interfere with the design of fate or even of kings. All in all, I think we'd be well advised to leave well alone." However, Rosencrantz is still not convinced: he objects that Hamlet has "done nothing to us." But Guildenstern asks that Rosencrantz apply neither logic nor a sense of justice at this moment, and Rosencrantz implicitly gives in, following up instead with a summary of events to this point, which leads us back to *Hamlet*, with Hamlet's rewriting of the letter to send Rosencrantz and Guildenstern to *their* deaths (110–111).

This is Rosencrantz's and Guildenstern's moment of present choice, their crisis, when they have the chance not just to act any predetermined story. As Gruber insists, "For a moment, *Hamlet* is swept away, suspended powerless; for a brief interim we sense that the fate of the prince and his play rests in Ros and Guil's hands. That interim is theirs alone; it does not belong to *Hamlet*. And they refuse to act. To choose not to choose, of course, is a manner of choosing" (306). Here Rosencrantz and Guildenstern effectively mimic Hamlet's decision not to heed his presentiment that the game with Laertes will lead his death, choosing "to leave well alone," or in this case, to "let be." Now they believe that in being on boat, "our movement is contained within a larger one that carries us along as inexorably as the wind and current" (122).[17]

Even though Shakespeare's text has the last word (although as the stage direction says, during that speech "the play fades, overtaken by dark and music" [126]), *Rosencrantz and Guildenstern* does not leave us certain as to whether it *is* an end. When the tragedians stage their final dumb show of multiple deaths including Rosencrantz's and Guildenstern's, Guildenstern protests, "No...no...no not for *us*, not like that. Dying is not romantic and death is not a game which will soon be over [...] It's the absence of presence, nothing more...the endless time of never coming back, a gap you can't see" (122). But they feel once again in temporal quandary, wondering "When did it begin?" and forgetting if there was ever a time when they did anything "wrong." Then in his final speech Guildenstern speculates that "there must have been a moment, at the beginning, when we could have said—no": no to the summons to the play, and implicitly, no to their collaboration in Hamlet's death (125). That there might indeed have been such a moment is underlined in his final words, which anticipate not the end, but a new beginning: "We'll know better next time. Now you see me, now you—(*And disappears*)" (125).[18] The audience would think that it is possible that the game which is the play can begin again, the coin tossed once more, with the potential always there that it could come up tails rather than heads, and where a choice could be made again.

This ending returns us to the beginning, where Rosencrantz and Guildenstern do indeed accept the invitation to participate. There they recount what happened "today," the banging on the shutters before dawn, the "royal summons," "the matter of extreme urgency" (19), and they respond to attend to an unknown task. Next, when they choose to engage with the players, they become participants rather than spectators. In this context Stoppard gestures several times at the play's audience, including them as participants in the present playing, gently pushing at rather than breaking down the fourth wall separating action and audience: for example, in Act 3 when Rosencrantz contemplates being seasick, they both "look out over the audience" and Guildenstern advises going upstage (101). At one moment, however, Rosencrantz directly demands the audience's participation. When Guildenstern contemplates the meaning of an order in which they are "condemned," Rosencrantz suddenly bellows "Fire!" at the house: he does so, he says, to demonstrate "the misuse of free speech. To prove that it exists. (*He regards the audience, that is the direction, with contempt,—and other directions, then front again.*) Not a move. They should burn to death in their shoes" (60). Stoppard here reminds the audience of their own complicity in the tragedy, as present spectators who have made the choice not to move, even though they may believe that speech is "free." Thomas Whitaker urges us to take away from this play the message that as "actors and witnesses of this play," we *can* act: even as we "maintain our spectatorial freedom," we can move "towards the condition of an author" (*Stoppard* 59–60).

RESCUING PENTHEUS: *DIONYSUS IN 69*

But how free is an audience as opposed to the actors of a play? Are spectators always defined by their passivity according to the conventions whereby the audience sits in the dark and responds to the show as asked, with laughter or tears? It is hard to forget Bertholt Brecht's description of modern audiences as "motionless figures in a peculiar condition: they seem strenuously to be tensing all their muscles, except where these are flabby and exhausted. [...] True, their eyes are open, but they stare rather than see, just as they listen rather than hear" (187). Brecht connects the audience's physical and mental passivity with the pleasures of tragic necessity itself:

> [T]he theatre as we know it shows the structure of society (represented on the stage) as incapable of being influenced by society (in the auditorium). Oedipus, who offended against certain principles underlying the society of his time, is executed: the gods see to that; they are beyond criticism. Shakespeare's great solitary figures, bearing on their breast the star of their fate, carry through with irresistible force their futile and deadly outbursts; they prepare their own downfall; life, not death, becomes obscene as they collapse; the catastrophe is beyond criticism. Human sacrifices all round! Barbaric delights! (189)

In Brecht's view, in witnessing tragedy, the audience and actors would appear to be locked in complicity in time as well as space, the audience knowing what is about to happen and never questioning if it could be any different.

But in reality, audiences are rarely as passive as the decorum of conventional theater dictates. Our cell phones ring despites all pleas to the contrary, our bodies assert themselves in coughing or even snoring, and we may laugh when we are meant to cry and stay silent when asked to respond. As Thomas Whitaker has described the balancing of agency among the parties that produce a play: "A spectator [...] is but an implicit actor; an actor can never fully realize his character; a character cannot really become his own author; and even an author is but a spectator of the action he creates. But each role also has its own advantages. Even a character can do much that is beyond the power of an author; an actor can know a freedom beyond that of his characters; and a spectator transcends the limitation of all action" (*Stoppard* 58). Whether or not actors and directors like it, audiences are implicitly essential partners in performance. They are not "model readers"; rather they function as unique "communities," responding actively and sometimes even with rage and riots when a performance has not been what they wanted or expected (see Carlson 13). Audience members can also simply walk out, refusing to play their roles. On many levels, an audience may thus consciously or unconsciously resist the narrative enacted on stage, in the "here and now" of their own bodies.[19]

Resistance is one form of audience response, but plays can also allow for the spectators to join in, or in the Player's words, "to get caught up in the action" (*Rosencrantz* 23). While the notion of audience participation exploded in the 1960s, the idea and practice are still very much alive today in the trend toward immersive theater, from "karaoke, role-playing games, tours of film industry theme parks in Florida, and theater productions such as *Tony n' Tina's Wedding*" (Freshwater, 58), as well as recent interactive performances like the Punchdrunk Theater Company's production of *Sleep No More*, based on *Macbeth*. In Gareth White's words, such performances "ask the spectator to speak or act in dialogue with the performers or the performance environ-ments, and to make choices that structure that experience" (2). Audience participation thus appears to empower the audience, imagining that, in Augusto Boal's feverish vision in *The Theater of the Oppressed*, "The spectator no longer delegates power to the characters either to think or to act in his place. The spectator frees himself; he thinks and acts for himself!" (122).[20]

Usually, active audience participation is limited to comic performance or to other forms of experimental theater in which the plots are not known in advance and thus are ripe for change. As Brecht suggests, traditional tragic performance would seem to require a passive audience, experiencing the anxiety and even the thrill of feeling helpless to prevent the catastrophe unfolding before them. Because I want to resist this assumption, I often return to an important exception to the rule, which occurred in the original run of Richard Schechner's Performance Group's staging of *Dionysus in 69*, their adaptation of Euripides's *Bacchae*. That production notoriously broke down boundaries between actors and spectators acting together in a potent present of enactment. We are fortunate that Brian de Palma recorded a version of the performance, and Schechner and the primary actors narrated its events in a book published in 1970. There is much to be said about that play's legendary run, but my focus will be those crises when, through the actors' and audience's choices, the tragic plot veered away from its expected end.[21]

In 1968, no play could have been more suitable for adaptation and recreation than Euripides's *Bacchae*.[22] Just as for Stoppard *Hamlet* was the apt text for exploring adaptation, playing, and the idea of tragedy, the *Bacchae* worked for Schechner and his company both because of its violence and sexuality and because the *Bacchae* stages a struggle for con-trol of the theater and life itself. Euripides's play does not categorically affirm tragic destiny or fate; rather it undermines it by showing how divine authority is imposed through violence. In his prologue Dionysus says he has returned to his birthplace Thebes to prove his divinity to those who deny it; he will do so by inspiring Agave to help murder her son Pentheus, the young king of Thebes. This Dionysus, son of a god and mortal, is not like Sophocles's gods, rendered invulnerable by their very absence from the scene. When we see Dionysus disguised as a priest (as an actor plays a role) while claiming to possess super powers, both the play's characters and the audience might defy him. By whose word do we know that he is a god, except his own and those of his followers?

Dionysus will indeed "prove" he is a god through inciting horrific violence among the women of Thebes, bringing Agave and her sisters to murder her son while in a Bacchic frenzy. As Cadmus says bitterly to Dionysus at the play's end, seeing Agave stroking the limbs of her dismembered son, "From all that you have done, it is clear to me you are a god" (298). But throughout the play, we see Dionysus, the god of tragedy, exercising power through performance that requires the audience's assent. In this, Euripides thus anticipates Plato's critique of tragedy's treacherous influence on a spectator who cannot distinguish illusion from reality and surrenders his or her reason. At a crucial moment, Dionysus is said to be imprisoned in Pentheus's palace, which would have been represented by the *skene*, the building behind the orchestra in the Athenian theater. Once he exits, the maenad chorus excitedly summons up the image of the palace collapsing:

> Dionysus is here in the hall!
> Revere him in awe!
> We do! We do!
> Do you see at the top of the columns, the lintels of stone,
> So high, that are breaking apart?
> Thundering Bromios is shouting
> His triumph from inside the house. (266)

While we do not know exactly how this was staged in the ancient theater, we can say confidently that the *skene* did not actually collapse.

So here the audience was explicitly asked to believe in Dionysus's power to destroy the palace, when they could see that nothing of the sort had happened. If the spectators did "believe," they in effect became one with the onstage participants who are also spectators, the chorus of Dionysus's followers from Asia. However, in pointing to the act of seeing, the chorus's call also creates a gap for skepticism. Charles Segal wonders if Euripides was thus asking whether "the power of Dionysus" is "something that can hypnotize us, the audience, into thinking that we can see something occur that has not in fact occurred (the collapse of the palace), or is it really a means of revealing the presence of divinity among men, or is it both together [...]?" (*Dionysiac Poetics*, 220). I think it is a moment to resist the power of Dionysus and his tragic plotting, if we consciously refuse to see it.

When adapting *The Bacchae* in *Dionysus in 69*, Schechner was deep into his experiment with what he called environmental theater. First, he argued, environmental theater demands the stripping of artifice, both the machinery of the theater and any illusion that dramatic characters are magically summoned out of nowhere. All of the actors who played Dionysus in this production self-consciously introduced themselves in their own person, as William Finley, Jason Bosseau, Patrick McDermott, or Joan MacIntosh, and then each announced that, as Dionysus, he or she had come to "announce my divinity." William Finley pointed to what that means for the audience: "Now for those of you who believe what I just told you, that I am a god, you are going to have a terrific evening. The rest of you are in trouble. It's going to be an hour and a half of being up against the wall. Those of you who do believe can join us in what we do next. It's a celebration, a ritual, and ordeal, an ecstasy."[23] The stakes are thus set high for the audience: comply with Dionysus throughout the playing time of the performance, or be in trouble by refusing to participate.[24]

Environmental theater also demanded that the performance experienced more as a "social event" rather than art, thus reaching for the "real" that embraces play by involving the audience in "real," extended present time. Because audience participation is always both unscripted and unrehearsed, Schechner argues, "participation is not about 'doing a play' but *undoing* it, transforming an aesthetic event into a social event—of shifting the focus from art-and-illusion to the potential or actual solidarity among everyone in the theater, performers and spectators alike" (*Environmental Theater* 45). What happens then potentially also undoes the idea that a play necessarily has a beginning, middle, and end; rather, it is constantly in the process of happening. In participatory theater, "*The contingencies of life that are the traditional subjects of drama suddenly become its object.* Will the play go on? How? Will it complete itself? How? What is my place in it? When there is participation, everyone in the theater tests destiny and gambles with fortune" (79, italics original). As Schechner's language suggests, this sort of theater can thus undermine the fundamentals of tragic necessity essential to the idea that a play must merely enact a preexisting text. Rather, in this theatrical experience that seems to exist in a continually unfolding present, "the text is a map with many possible routes; it is also a map than can be redrawn" (xliv).

As a tragedy that itself experiments with the audience's and characters' compulsion to "give in" as the action happens, the *Bacchae* thus made a potent vehicle for the Performance Group's experimentation with participation. Their adaptation was a pastiche of several Greek tragedies, using about half of William Arrowsmith's translation of the *Bacchae* along with some lines from *Antigone* and *Hippolytus*, the rest was written by the performers. While Schechner says the performances themselves were not improvised, the actors playing the main roles all composed different versions of their lines, so there were multiple variants of the script. With these variations, Schechner reports that at most performances the action happened more or less according to what he calls his "game-plan" (78). Indeed, we can think of *Dionysus in 69*, like *Rosencrantz and Guildenstern*, as the quintessential theatrical game, which allows for play and variation within its basic plot structure. But at several memorable performances participation and improvisation disrupted the Group's plan, when both performers and spectators felt that in a crisis they could make a choice to act with consequences.

Accounts of the run of *Dionysus* indicate that many people attended the play several times, so that those whose knew the play could "enter it at any of several places and change the flow of the action," where the changes were "modular—in tone, speed, intensity. Even those who are at the performance for the first time can participate if they stick to the rules" (Schechner, *Performance Theory* 57). But Schechner also relates two times when people did not play "by the rules." One involved the audience's intervention. As Schechner tells the story:

One night a bunch of students from Queens College kidnapped Pentheus, preventing his sacrifice to Dionysus. As they seized him, William Shephard, playing Pentheus, went limp, and Jason Bosseau, playing Dionysus, jumped between the students and the theater door. A fierce argument raged between Bosseau/Dionysus and the students. "You came here with a plan all worked out!" he shouted. They agreed and said, "Why not?" Arguments broke out among many spectators not of few of whom thought the whole thing was rigged by the Group. This contingent cynically whined, "Come on now, we've had enough of this, get on with the play we paid money to see!" Finally Pentheus was carried from the theater and unceremoniously dumped on Grand Street. He refused to come back and resume the performance. (*Environmental Theater* 41)

The performers and audience thus reached an impasse, where it seemed as if the play could not continue. The problem was solved only when an experienced audience volunteer agreed to play Pentheus's role, improvising the lines. As Schechner's account suggests, at stake in this encounter was what is "planned" and by whom: by Euripides, Dionysus, Schechner, or the rebellious students. Schechner reports that he was "elated that something 'real' had happened," and he himself did not contest the students' right to have a plan: why not, since he himself had one? (41). Ironically, the audience members were the ones who insisted that the play go on and the punishment of Pentheus continue in the person of one of their own; they were too invested in the outcome that they had paid to witness.

In contrast, at another time, it was the actor playing Pentheus (again, William Shephard) who resisted his entrapment in the plot. As the performance careened toward the catastrophe, Dionysus always offered Pentheus "any woman in the room." Sometimes a woman in the audience would step forth, but this scene usually ended with the woman's rejecting Pentheus, and Pentheus's proceeding to his slaughter. But as Shephard reports, on one night the emotional interaction was so intense that he felt as if he were "lifted [...] out of the play, as though someone had grabbed me by the hair and pulled me up to the ceiling. I looked around and I saw the garage and the other actors, and I said, 'It finally happened.' The play fell away, like shackles being struck from my hands. The way the play is set up, Pentheus is trapped inside its structure. But on that night it all seemed to fall away and I walked out the door."[25] Joan MacIntosh, the woman playing Dionysus that night, duly reported Pentheus's victory and the play's end to the audience. Later, however, she confessed her sense of being "betrayed" (thus echoing the language of infidelity or lack of faithfulness we have seen associated with adaptation) (Schechner, *Performance Theory* 52–3; see also *Dionysus in 69*). Whereas Shephard celebrated his own power to escape the play's tragic prison, in contrast, while playing a Dionysus invested in the catastrophe MacIntosh felt abandoned. For both Shephard and MacIntosh, this moment called for the breaking of the bond of faith that demands belief in the play and the god's illusory force.

An actress who played Agave, Ciel Smith, has described the play's crisis as taking the form of a deadly game, one of life and death: "A life wager lies dormant in the middle of our play. Every night Pentheus is left alone in the center, weighing the balance between self and actor. He tries to peel away the actor until the person stands exposed. There is a chance the wager will be won and the play end then" (*Dionysus in 69*). She relates how one night she felt that "I, like Bill, should have an opportunity to save myself from the inevitability of my role and my action," and so she refused to participate in killing Pentheus. However, she says, the play "continued and concluded without my killing." In the end, she was only a player who could be replaced or supplemented within the rules of the game.

What happened on those nights in *Dionysus in 69* was admittedly a rare occurrence, ripping open the agonizing tension of what Smith called the "wager," which is also the game of both the *Bacchae* and *Dionysus in 69*. Schechner reflected that in the case of this play "it is hard to build into a performance both narrative power and the tensions of a sporting match. The two ambitions cross each other" (*Performance Theory* 53). That is, as a story the play needed to move toward its catastrophe and conclusion; however, as a game, a wager, or "sporting match," it had to appear that the outcome was uncertain. It is the same conflict built into the coin toss in *Rosencrantz and Guildenstern*: even if in one framework the outcome looks rigged, the game can be played over and over again, in the hope that the coin can and will fall anew. Once again, the game gives the idea of tragedy all away.

Dionysus in 69 thus represents an extreme version of undoing tragedy through adaptive performance, in contrast to *Rosencrantz and Guildenstern's* cooler and more ironic version of adaptation as intervention. On the one hand, in its visceral forms of participation, *Dionysus in 69* was meant to inspire the ecstasy of submission to Bacchic frenzy and thus submission to the story Dionysus wants to tell. But on the other hand, in calling attention to its own imposition of illusions, and to the interplay of present, lived, and mythic temporalities, it revealed the consequences of submission and generated resistance to them. *Rosencrantz and Guildenstern* relies more on sustaining the environment of playful uncertainty, a sense of a present game world in which the coin is suspended in the air, before it falls. What both of them have in common is a twisting of tragic temporality, in manipulating the idea of tragic "present time" in the temporality of the game that is performance. *Rosencrantz and Guildenstern* creates a kind of indeterminate "present" within the playing time of *Hamlet*, where choices may still be made. The environmental theater of *Dionysus in 69* converted the onrush of tragic temporality into a different kind of "real time" for the audience and actors alike, a time not governed by the play's plot, and in which choice is still free. Both plays excite the players' and the audience's desire to see and experience that moment of freedom from the story, to make a difference, just in time.

NOTES

1. See Fuchs's introduction to *The Death of Character* on the emphasis on "presence" in the theater of the 1970s and its breakdown in most post-modern theater and performance (Fuchs 1996). On the time of the "present" in theater, see Wagner, Chap. 1 (Wagner 2014); Richardson (Richardson 1987); and Maisano on how in the theater "'now' is nothing but a repetition, representation, mediation, and interpretation of time" (385) (Maisano 2013).
2. See Harris on how "the stagecraft of the King's Men—their acting styles, special effects, and stage properties" was "untimely" (20): that is, each object, movement, sound, body had its own history, interwoven into the actions of the present (Harris 2011).
3. On "Original Practices" see Steigerwalt (Steigerwalt 2013).
4. See also Sack 27 (Sack 2015).
5. See Kidnie on how "precisely what constitutes authentic Shakespeare is a question that can never finally be resolved since there is not an *a priori* category that texts or staging are a production *of* [...] The issue is therefore not how performance departs from or otherwise adapts text, but the shifting criteria by which both texts and performances are recognized—or not—as instances of a certain work" (9–10) (Kidnie 2008). See also Lavender on the instability of the text and early modern performance practice and its consequences for "Shakespeare reworked" (Lavender 2001).
6. In considering the relationship between performance and adaptation, Kidnie has challenged the notion of performance as having a "second order status" where "performance is measured in relation to the text in degrees of *in*fidelity and *in*authenticity" (104) (Kidnie 2005).
7. See Hutcheon: "Adaptations are obviously not new to our time, however; Shakespeare transferred his culture's stories from page to stage and made them available to a whole new audience. Aeschylus and Racine and Goethe and da Ponte also retold familiar stories in new forms. Adaptations are so much a part of Western culture that they appear to affirm Walter Benjamin's insight that 'storytelling is always the art of repeating stories'" (2) (Hutcheon and O'Flynn 2013). Also see Sanders on Shakespeare as an "active adapter and imitator" (46) (Sanders 2006).

8. Gilbert and Tompkins argue further that "even in the face of fixed dialogue and/or plot closure, manipulation of a play's performative codes and contexts can productively shift the power structures that seem predetermined in the originary script" (19) (Gilbert and Tompkins 1996).

9. See Sanders: "Adaptation and appropriation [...] supplementing, complementing, coming after Derrida and Darwin [...] are all about multiple interactions and a matrix of possibilities" (60) (Sanders 2006).

10. See Berlin on *Rosencrantz and Guildenstern* as an act of criticism itself (Berlin 1973).

11. Bradby notes that "we are left with nothing but what Geneviève Serreau termed 'le jeu pur' ('pure play')" (Bradby 2001); see also Serreau, 90 (Serreau 1996). Also see Bradby on ways in which "the theme of being in time is *experienced* by characters and audiences alike" (26) (Bradby 2001).

12. On time in *Waiting for Godot*, see Schechner, "There's Lots of Time in Godot" (who also relates time in *Godot* to games) (Schechner 1966) and Wagner, 21–22 (Wagner 2014).

13. See States, *Shape of Paradox*: when speculating on the day of the week, Estragon "is squandering time, putting the play outside of all temporal reality while seeming to be immersed in its categories" (35) (States 1978).

14. As States observes, "the failure of memory in Beckett [...] is [...] a built-in convenience by which the play is able to escape all moorings in time and space that might lock the characters into a causal history" (35) (States 1978).

15. Schechner, in "There's Lots of Time in Godot," discusses gaming and time in *Godot* (Schechner 1996); Whitaker notes the omnipresence of "theatre games" in *Rosencrantz and Guildenstern* (63) (Whitaker 1983).

16. In general, see Costikyan, who emphasizes the importance of uncertainty in games. He argues that "part of the reason games appeal is because they allow us to explore uncertainty"—even if the end is fixed (13) (Costikyan 2013). That openness is reinforced through the agonistic game that Rosencrantz and Guildenstern later play bandying questions, a give-and-take that parodies Vladimir's and Estragon's verbal gameplaying, whether in their game of escalating insults or efforts at conversation ("Come on, Gogo, *return the ball*, can't you, once in a way," says Vladimir [6]).

17. See also Keyssar-Franke on the question of Rosencrantz's and Guildenstern's relative freedom to act: she sees them given a chance to play but ultimately entrapped within the plot of *Hamlet* and idea of destiny (Keyssar-Franke 1975). Whitaker also sees that "as lively reflectors on their destiny, Rosencrantz and Guildenstern are bound neither by Shakespeare's plot nor by our usual dullness of speech and imagination. To the very end they are able to rise into a spectatorial freedom and a quasi-authorial creativity" (59) (Whitaker 1983). See also Schlueter on "the illusion of choice" in the play (74) (Schlueter 1995).

18. But see Gruber on the ending of *Rosencrantz and Guildenstern*: "in rehearsals and in all published editions of the play after the first, Stoppard excised a bit of action which brought his drama full circle, so that it ended with someone banging on a shutter shouting two names" (91) (Gruber 1981–1982).

19. See Blau for a comprehensive study of the idea of the audience (Blau 1990). See also Freshwater who discusses the often-vexed relationship between players, directors, actors, and audience (Freshwater 2009). See Low and Myhill on the agency of audience in early modern period (Low and Myhill 2011).

20. Freshwater provides an important critique of assumptions about participation and agency (70) (Freshwater 2009). See also Blau on the "participation mystique" (Blau 1990).

21. On the performance of *Dionysus in 69* as "a landmark in the history of the reception of Greek theatre in the twentieth century," see Zeitlin, "Dionysus in 69" (51) (Zeitlin 2004).

22. On other adaptations of the *Bacchae*, see Hall et al. (2004).

23. There are no page numbers in this text.

24. Finley as Dionysus also said to Shephard as Pentheus: "Bill, you don't understand. You're a man. I'm a god. This is a tragedy. The odds are against you."

25. Victor Turner recounts Schechner's rehearsal of Ibsen's *A Doll House* where "we came up with four Noras, one of whom actually made a choice contrary to Ibsen's script. It happened that in her personal life she herself was being confronted with a dilemma similar to Nora's. [...] Eventually, instead of detonating the famous door slam that some critics say ushered in modern theater, she rushed back to the group, signifying that she was not ready—at least not yet—to give up her children, thus throwing unexpected light on the ethical toughness of Ibsen's Nora" (88) (Turner 1982).

CHAPTER 3

Time-Travel Films: Replaying Time, Choice, and Action

Abstract This chapter follows resistance to the tragic narrative in the medium of film, exemplified in those films that involve travel through time, when the protagonist pursues a desire to see a story undone by revisiting a past tragic choice or event. These films play on or with that impulse to resist the script's authority inherent in acts of adaptation, and they translate it into a character's defiance of social or political authority in a quest to right a wrong, to prevent a future disaster, or recover what has been lost. The script's authority is identified with a sense of the inexorable nature of time, which film itself has the power to undermine it. The first part considers films (including *La Jétee, 12 Monkeys, Déjà Vu,* and *Looper*) that set time travel in an socio-political framework, in which a male time traveler must disobey the authorities that send him back in time. These models are then contrasted with *Run Lola Run* and *Céline and Julie Go Boating*, films that feature female protagonists who use a time-loop or game-like structure to transform a tragic outcome into a comic ending. Time travel thus lends itself to the conversion of narrative into a game, when the linearity of time is twisted through recursion and repetition.

Keywords Time · Temporality · Choice · Crisis · Tragedy · Drama · Fate · Film · Cinema · Time travel · Games · Videogames · Play · *Céline and Julie Go Boating* · *Run Lola Run* · Jacques Rivette · Terry Gilliam · Chris Marker · Tom Tykwer · *Source Code* · *12 Monkeys* · *La Jetée* · *Looper* · *Déjà Vu* · Time loop

© The Author(s) 2016
R. Bushnell, *Tragic Time in Drama, Film, and Videogames,*
DOI 10.1057/978-1-137-58526-4_3

Theatrical performance and adaptation can feed a need to imagine that a script can be altered, or in Richard Schechner's words, "undone," even when that undoing threatens to frustrate the expectations that we bring to the theater in the first place (*Environmental Theater* 45). Performance and adaptation recognize that there is as much pleasure in resisting a story's authority as in seeing our expectations fulfilled. This chapter follows this idea of resistance to the narrative in a different medium, that of film, as exemplified in films that involve travel through time, when the protagonist pursues a desire to see a story undone by revisiting a past tragic choice or event.[1] These films play on or with that impulse to resist the script's authority inherent in acts of adaptation, and they translate it into a character's defiance of social or political authority in a quest to right a wrong, to prevent a future disaster, or recover what has been lost. The script's authority is identified with a sense of the inexorable nature of time, which film itself has the power to undermine.

Focusing on a small set of representative films, this chapter investigates how cinematic time-travel experiments with the temporality of the medium itself to unravel the model of tragic temporality. My first topic will be films that set time travel in an socio-political framework, in which a male time traveler must disobey the authorities that send him back in time. In so doing, the films set up a contest between the male traveler and time that often requires heroic self-sacrifice; a happy ending comes about only through the fantasy of an alternate universe. I then contrast these films with two featuring female protagonists who instead use a time-loop or game-like structure to transform a tragic ending into a comic one. Time travel thus lends itself to the feminist conversion of narrative into a game in which the linearity of time is twisted through recursion and repetition.

Traveling in the Present and Past

The wildly popular genre of time-travel films can be roughly divided into two types: those that involve projection into the future and those in which the traveler returns to the past to try to reverse some disastrous event. In all of them past, present, and future are intricately intertwined. In some films it seems that the lives of all humanity are at stake: so, for example, the *Terminator* films stage a human battle against the machines, in which the only hope lies in saving the future's hero. In *La Jetée* time travel imports essential future technology into a post-apocalyptic present (although it cannot prevent the time-traveler's death). The outcome is similar in Terry

Gilliam's *12 Monkeys* (based on *La Jetée*), which also kills off the time-traveling hero Cole but allows him to bring the secret of a deadly pandemic virus from the past into the future to provide the basis for the cure. Many time-travel films also mix personal desires into this story of heroic rescue. In *Déjà Vu*, federal agent Doug Carlin travels back in time to avert both a terrorist explosion and the death of a woman he has come to love. In *Source Code*, the Army soldier Stevens is sent back repeatedly to the past to prevent a disaster, but he also saves a woman he has met there. In *Run Lola Run*, Lola is able to reverse time twice, first to undo her own death and then to save her boyfriend Manni.

Time-travel films thus connect us to both terror about future disasters unknown and fear of loss in the past. As Constance Penley has noted, time-travel films tend to represent huge catastrophic endings (78–80), like the *Terminator* films' world of the machines, *12 Monkeys'* life after a global pandemic, or *Donnie Darko*'s collapse of the universe because of a temporal anomaly. But often at the story's heart lies the male time-traveler's love for a woman encountered in the past.[2] (*Run Lola Run* reverses this phenomenon in having its female protagonist rescue her hapless boyfriend.) Jacqueline Furby describes this phenomenon as the "Orphic rescue fantasy" of time-travel films that "add the element of redemption and involve a cyclical movement of return and change. If movies are slices of the past reanimated, or visions of alternative worlds, into which the time traveling spectator is drawn, then they represent the perfect medium for the exploration of nostalgic return rescue narratives" (78).[3]

Even as both the traveler's and audience's view shifts between past and future, a sense of present time or crisis usually tightly constrains his or her experience. Lola has only twenty minutes to save Manni; in *Source Code* Stevens must race against the clock to prevent a second explosion; in *Back to the Future Part 1*, Marty has only a few minutes to get back to the present and rescue Doc before the lightning strikes the clock tower. Clocks are everywhere in time-travel films, counting down the minutes passing until the catastrophe that the time traveler must prevent. Even when time has been bent, both audience and characters experience entrapment in a temporality of crisis that echoes the tragic crisis; the traveler must act in another time against time.

The cinematic time-traveler's struggle thus becomes both a conflict with the past and its story and a struggle with time, using time against itself. And why not, in what Maya Deren would call this "time form" (154), this medium that captures moments in the past but streams out before viewers as if it were ever present? Echoing Alain Robbe-Grillet, many film scholars have noted the strange presentness of film (see Cardwell 82), which at first seems to echo theatrical performance.[4] In observing that "time travel depends on the notion that all events are somehow present," where from some viewpoint "all instants are simultaneous," Bruce Kawin reminds us that "one of the simplest and most convincing images for this concept of time is the reel of film," on which "thousands of frames maintain their images of *potential* instants, all together and retrievable" and thus "give the impression of 'happening now'" (16, italics original).

Gilles Deleuze has taken the opposite view, agreeing with Jean-Luc Godard that the image exists in the present only in bad films (38). Of course, like the photograph, the film image can never be fully present, for it is a record of an action and place captured at another time. In *The Emergence of Cinematic Time*, Mary Anne Doane points to the paradoxical temporality of the film image:

> Once the present as contingency has been seized and stored, it ineluctably becomes the past. Yet this archival artifact becomes strangely immaterial; existing nowhere but in its screening for a spectator in the present, it becomes the experience of presence (this is the sense in which film is usually associated with the present tense rather than the past). What is archived, then, would be the experience of presence. But it is the disjunctiveness of a presence relived, of a presence haunted by historicity. (23)

All films are in this sense documentary, even as they present themselves as fictions. Whatever appeared in front the camera existed once, however "fake" at the time.

While film thus implicitly involves the experience of the past in the present, that present effect relies on our willingness to believe that what we are seeing happens in "real" time. We know (although we easily forget) that cinematic scenes consist of fragments filmed out of sequence and then reassembled to produce the sense of continuous time. Viewers of classic films accept the conventions of the dissolve and fade, which point to time's passage but do not disrupt the sense of moving forward. However, unlike everyday time and theatrical time, cinematic time can be stretched or compressed, slowed down, speeded up or even reversed through the unique qualities of the medium.[5] In Furby's words, in this sense, "nearly all cinematic narratives involve a kind of time travel as they reshuffle and reorder time, stretch and shrink duration, and alter the frequency of events" (77). Film thus both suggests and enables the time-travel narrative.[6]

Because of this unique temporality, film has the capacity to reinvent the tragic moment in a different way from performance. Gilles Deleuze has described cinematic temporality as a condition in which "there is no present which is not haunted by a past and a future, by a past which is not reducible to a former present, by a future which does not consist of a present to come" (37). The analogies with tragic temporality as described in Chap. 1 are clear: film materializes the present contingencies of crisis, in which action takes place or a choice must be made, drawing in past, present, and future. Yet in that materiality, film opens up time, and thus choice, to manipulation in which the present, past, and future can be confused.

FILM AS TIME TRAVEL

How do people travel through time in movies? Many films draw on the idea that the traveler needs some sort of technology to do so, beginning with H.G. Wells' invention of a time machine made "of nickel, parts of ivory, parts [that] had certainly been filed or sawn out of rock crystal" (*Time Machine* 11; see also Nahin 13). While sometimes the travelers drive to the past (memorably, in the DeLorean of the *Back to the Future* series), most often they are inserted into something resembling a space capsule found in a laboratory bristling with electronics.[7] Less noticed, however, are the ways in which sight and the camera can signal time travel, linking the control of time with photography and filmmaking itself.[8]

In *La Jetée* scientists trigger the journey to the past by injecting a substance and applying a blindfold with electrodes over the time-traveler's eyes, connecting the travel to sight. Representing events of past, present, and future, the film is composed of a sequence of photographic stills, except for one brief moment of live action, when the eyes of the traveler's lover flutter open. While Janet Harbord has written of *La Jetée* that it allows cinema to be both a "document, inscription of time" and a montage indicating "a complete irreverence for time" (23), cinema in *La Jetée* is also sight *in* time: a fragmented yet continuous reality, playing with the camera's eye. At the same time that he sees the past, the time traveler in *La Jetée* is seen by a scientist who trails him wearing strange goggles. As Bruce Kawin comments on the film's ending, "the narrator's summation, that 'one cannot escape from time,' might without distortion be rephrased 'one cannot escape from film'" (16). *Twelve Monkeys* explicitly develops *La Jetée*'s technology of surveillance as part of the conditions of time travel; visiting the past means both watching and being watched. The time-traveler Cole receives his mission in a laboratory dominated by an outlandish machine shaped like an eye encrusted with different video screens, one staring directly at him.[9] We come to understand that the future authorities who have designed his mission can somehow watch him. Instead of sight as the means of travel, in this film the camera becomes an omnipresent metaphor for control of time and the traveler himself.

Sometimes time-travel films will foreground camera effects and sometimes they will disguise them, thus influencing the viewer's sense of the "reality" of the time represented. In *Déjà Vu*, scientists have invented a surveillance technology to see *in* the past anew (hence the title), with a gap of approximately four and a half days: as one of the characters puts it, one can thus follow a "single trailing moment of now in the past." Using that camera to track the ferryboat bomber, Carlin and the agents become directors, panning and zooming as they search for clues in the past, with the legend "lens adjusting" often superimposed on the screen within the screen. When Carlin goes out in the field with a hand-held version of the camera, both in the past and yet not in the past, time travel becomes literally a kind of filmmaking. Once the bomber has been found and arrested after the fact, the authorities want Carlin to stop, but he wishes to *really* go back, this time to prevent the catastrophe. Once he does enter the past, he needs no camera, and the earlier special cinematic effects largely dissipate (except for slow motion), producing a stronger illusion of the unmediated "reality" of this new story being created in the past. When Carlin prevents the explosion and saves Claire, that version of events seems more "real" than the reality conveyed in the first two sections of the film, where filmmaking is always on display. The time traveler has in effect seized control of the time invested in film itself.

Tom Tykwer has said that in *Run Lola Run* he wanted to convey that 35-mm film embodies a sense of "real time" and of reality itself. He compared "the sequences with Lola and Manni [...] shot on 35 mm" with the others "shot on video—in kind of a synthetic, artificial world." So, Twyker claims that effect "places Lola and Manni at the center of their world, in which miracles can happen just like in the movies. The film image is true, and the others are untrue, as it were. So when Lola runs through a video image, it becomes film" ("Director's Statement"). Tykwer here appears to grant film not only qualities of presence and truth, but also a potentiality, "where miracles can happen." As the character identified with film, Lola is indeed powerful; she is also, implicitly, the character who can control time, who can shatter clocks with her scream and start the movie all over again. Even as her actions reach into the realm of the unreal, Tykwer invests the power of film in her will.

While manipulating time, time-travel films thus identify the control of time with the camera and its ability to create present reality effects. Time-travel films represent different periods of time past and present as inherently in conflict, raising the question for the spectators of which we are to accept as "real" in the end. As was the case with the audiences of the *Bacchae* and *Dionysus in 69*, the spectators of the time-travel film are subject to the call to believe in what they see enacted before them. While time-travel films may draw attention to the medium of sight as the traveler journeys to the past, in the end, if the spectators are to trust that the traveler has succeeded in his or her mission to change the past, they must also submit to film's insistence on its own presence and its power.

CHOICE AND RESISTANCE IN TIME

If time travel is predicated on the possibility of escaping linear temporality, what happens to the decisive moment, the context for the choice which changes everything? As I have suggested above, characteristically, a crisis does frame travel in time, creating tension by limiting the amount of time allotted to the hero to save the day (as it were). For example, *12 Monkeys* ends with a race in what it appears to be "real time" to catch the terrorist with the virus before he gets on a plane. *Source Code* deals with several kinds of time pressure: the eight minutes Stevens has on the train to discover the bomber; the ticking clock of the overarching story, measuring the hours before the next explosion; and finally, the short interval in which Stevens' operator, Captain Goodwin, must decide whether to send Stevens back in time once more and then let him die.

The suspense created by this limited time often frames the male traveler's resistance to his mission. In many films a futuristic state or unnamed power has ordered the traveler to pursue a criminal or to save a future world from disaster: in *12 Monkeys*, Cole is a prisoner of the state, like the nameless prisoner in *La Jetée*; in *Source Code*, Stevens is essentially only a brain and a heart trapped on life support and is thus powerless; and in *Déjà Vu*, Carlin is told just to do his job. For these characters, the significant choice entails ultimately defying those authorities that have directed their mission from the first, when they choose to pursue a personal goal by remaining in the past or dying in an attempt to change it.

One strategy makes that act of disobedience an essential part of the plot itself, in effect replicating the logic of a tragic scenario in which an effort to avert prophecy comes to fulfill it. Full of adolescent angst and rebellion but haunted by the idea that he has a mission, Donnie Darko asks his physics teacher if one can see into the future. The teacher replies: "If we could see our destinies manifest themselves visually [...] then we would be given the choice to betray our chosen destinies. The very fact that this choice would exist [...] would mean that all preferred destinies would end." But Donnie demurs: "Not if you chose to stay within God's channel"—where "channel" suggests both the film's omnipresent television broadcasts and the flows of plasma that represent Donnie's capacity to see into future time. That is, Donnie accepts that whatever he chooses may be providential. In *La Jetée*, too, the time-traveler's choice to defy authority is understood to have always been part of the story. The people of the future offer him the opportunity to stay there, but he requests instead to return to the past, which brings him to the jetty at Orly where once again he glimpses the woman he loves. But as he runs toward her, he understands that "on ne s'évade pas du Temps"—one cannot escape time, when he is shot by one of the scientists from his present, the very death he witnessed as a child.

Twelve Monkeys adapts this scenario by explicitly associating entrapment in linear time with social and political obedience. Cole's decision to remain in the past occurs in the film's middle, when he opts to stay with Dr. Railly, his lover, who convinces him to still try to prevent the spread of the virus. When they are chasing the villain at the airport, another agent from the future attempts to stop them. He tells Cole: "Point of fact—you don't belong here. It's not permitted to let you stay." Cole replies: "This is the present. This is not the past. This is not the future. This is right now!" However, the agent responds, "Look, I got orders, man! You know what I'm supposed to do if you don't go along? I'm supposed to shoot the lady! You got that? They said, 'If Cole don't obey this time, Garcia, you gotta shoot his girlfriend!' ... I got no choice, man. These are my orders." And Cole understands, "This part isn't about the virus, is it? ... It's about obeying, about doing what you're told." Cole thus chooses to remain in the present in which he is acting at that moment in the film, which he (like the viewer) does not immediately perceive as the past as the film rolls on before us. Like the protagonist of *La Jétee*, in the end, when Cole attempts to change the past, he is assassinated: the terrorist boards the plane with his virus, while we see him joined by one of the scientists of the future, in an ambiguous ending. Insofar as we want to imagine the actions played out before us as the present, Cole's choice appears to be "free," framed as disobedience to the future authorities communicating through their agents. At the same time, as in *La Jetée*, the audience comes to understand that this resistance must be accepted as part of the story of the past, replaying the death scene Cole remembers witnessing as a child. It is an act in which the film's present coincides with the past, and it is a closed loop, identifying the linearity of time with a kind of tyranny, even if we may be reassured that now the future will be better.

Such repressive scenarios for time travel thus link the success of the male traveler's mission to save humankind from disaster to self-sacrifice. They posit that the traveler's choice is free and an act of rebellion in the present while it is also contained in the plot of the past. The ambiguity of *12 Monkeys'* ending however, is characteristic of many time-travel films' wanting to leave the viewer with some kind of hope. For example, *Looper* implies that a rebellious choice of self-sacrifice might indeed change everything. In this film's twisted plot, the shadowy authorities of a dystopian future ruled by a "Rainmaker" send people they wish to eliminate into the past to be executed by "loopers," who are themselves destroyed if they fail to complete their missions. One looper, whom I will call "Old Joe," is sent back to be executed by his younger self, but he escapes. He then undertakes a quest to find and kill the child who will become the "Rainmaker," the tyrant responsible for this disastrous future world and Joe's own wife's death. At the film's end, the younger Joe sees Old Joe about to shoot Sarah, the mother protecting that child. The younger Joe has a vision that if he saves Sarah, her child will not grow up psychologically damaged and thus not become the Rainmaker. With Old Joe out of his weapon's range, he must choose either to let Sarah be killed or to kill himself, thus eliminating his older self and saving Sarah. As the narrator says, in younger Joe's voice: "I saw it and the past was a circle round and round, so I changed it." The film leaves open the question of how his choice will in fact make a difference—except that here the narrator uses the past tense, in contrast to the film's opening, where the voiceover begins in the present.[10]

More often, however, popular time-travel films seem to recognize that audiences would resist the notion of the protagonist's necessary submission to time. The more palatable way of resolving the philosophical dilemmas of changing the past resorts to the fantasy of alternate realities, made possible by the notion of multiple universes.[11] As Elana Gomel has observed, if we do not worry too much about the physics, the alternate reality allows the time traveler to "have his cake and eat it, to believe that 'Time is only a kind of Space' and yet that the will is free, that agency matters, and that meaningful change is possible" (349). The existence of multiple universes enables both dramatic self-sacrifice and a "happy ending" without generating logical contradictions.[12] For example, in *Source Code*, when Stevens receives his mission to identify the train bomber, he is told that his job is just to prevent a future bombing, not to eradicate the past one. His supervisors tell him that "out here"—that is, in the frame "present"—"the clock only moves in one direction." But after the bomber is caught, Stevens insists that he *can* go back in the past, and make a difference; then he wants to die, defying his superior who wants to keep him alive to complete similar missions. Captain Goodwin, Stevens' operator and link to the world, makes the critical decision in time. "It's your choice," Stevens says (after asking whether her life might have been different if she had made different choices). When her boss is absent, she has just a few minutes to decide, and then she both sends him back and disconnects his life support. But this time, we see him preventing the first explosion and connecting with the girl he has rescued, in a parallel universe.[13] In a similar way, in *Déjà Vu*, Carlin can thwart the ferry explosion and save Claire, but only through his own self-sacrifice and death; however, the film inexplicably ends happily with his meeting Claire at the ferry dock as the agent investigating the averted catastrophe. He does not recognize her, but she knows him; somehow these two worlds touch or overlap with each other.

In *Narrative and Freedom: The Shadows of Time*, Gary Saul Morson registers his concern about the ethics of the narrative construction of multiple universes, where if "every contingent event is enacted in some universe, there are no unactualized possibilities and all choices are made." Morson first worries about what this means for the construction of character: how, he asks, can we explain the formation of identity in multiple universes, "insofar as identity depends on what we choose and what we forego, what happens if nothing is forgone?" Further, Morson argues, in multiple universes the moral hazards of choice are undone: "because all choices are made somewhere, the totality of good and evil in existence becomes a zero-sum game." Finally, Morson observes, "and most strangely, the fact that possibilities do not exceed actualities reintroduces determinism by a new and unexpected route. Everything that happens had to happen, and nothing that could have taken place failed to take place." In multiple universes, "choice loses much of its significance insofar as the significance of choice depends on its singularity and on what possibilities were left unactualized" (232–33). Morson's concerns about the ultimate loss of the meaning of choice would certainly extend to popular time-travel films like *Source Code* and *Déjà Vu* that imply the existence of multiple universes to bridge tragedy and comedy. Unlike the more uncompromising *La Jetée, 12 Monkeys,* and *Donnie Darko,* these films provide the appealing heroics of the ethical choice of self-sacrifice and the finality of the tragic death along with an ending in which the protagonist escapes the story forever. Disobeying authority does break open a new place and new time, created by the protagonists out of the materials of past time, but only by paralleling the tragic scenario rather than transforming it.

REPLAYING TIME OVER AND OVER AGAIN

An alternative version of redemptive cinematic time travel is the time-loop narrative, in which the protagonist goes repeatedly back to the past, learns from the experience, and transforms the story. The quintessential time-loop film is the comic *Groundhog Day,* in which, by rehearsing a single day for what may be decades, the broadcaster Phil Connors learns to become the person who can successfully woo the woman he desires. But the time-loop mechanism also surfaces in films with a potentially tragic or dramatic frame in which a character has limited time to learn how to avert a catastrophe: for example, in those repeated eight minutes that Stevens has to find the bomber in *Source Code.* Similarly, in *Live, Die Repeat: Edge of Tomorrow,* the combat-inexperienced army officer William Cage is caught in a time loop where he must die repeatedly in order to win the epic battle against aliens, using his knowledge of the future to develop new skills and strategies. As Victor Navarro-Remesal and Sheila García-Catalán have commented, "Diegetically, the time loop becomes a problem-solving process; extradiegetically, it reveals the inner workings of the media formats and genres of these stories in a metadiscursive manner": that is, while it is a strategy to advance a story, it also relies on and exposes film's ability to repeat and modify itself (206–7).

In undoing tragic necessity, this time-loop model offers an ethically different approach to choice in time and consequences. It adapts the structure of performative play and games to the time-travel scenario, offering the pleasure of interrupting a linear narrative. In contrast to my earlier examples of time-travel film that feature self-sacrificing men, my two case studies of time looping, Jacques Rivette's *Céline and Julie Go Boating* (*Céline et Julie vont en bateau*) and Tom Tykwer's *Run Lola Run* (*Lola rennt*), portray female protagonists who interrupt the tragic narrative of choice and consequence in time through adaptation. Both films appropriate the male "Orphic rescue fantasy" to depict how comic repetition and improvisation can interfere in the tragic plot. These films develop the kind of present temporality of play and games embedded in participatory performance, while they also anticipate or reflect the radical reconstruction of temporality characteristic of videogames, the subject of my next chapter.

Céline and Julie Go Boating is a dazzling demonstration of playful—and performative—undoing of tragedy through a form of time travel.[14] During one Parisian summer the two eponymous protagonists discover and comically infiltrate a tragedy enacted in a mysterious old house. Adapted from Henry James' *The Other House* (as well as his short story "The Certain Romance of Old Clothes"), that fusty-looking, archly acted tragedy involves two women, Sophie and Camille, competing for the love of the insufferable Olivier, a drama that climaxes in the unexplained death of a child, Madlyn. This scenario also seems to parallel an event in Julie's childhood; it thus represents the past in both a literary sense, through the form of the James story, and a diegetic sense, in suggesting a back story for the women's lives. At first, Céline and Julie each enter and exit the house alone, apparently playing a role in the tragedy as the child's nurse, Miss Angèle. When they leave, they recall the events witnessed there as film clips, in a fragmented and hallucinatory fashion. While at first amused by the story's absurdities, they come to realize that Madlyn's life is at stake, although they do not know who commits the murder. In a variation of the time-travel rescue fantasy, they conclude, "We have no choice. We must do something. We must save the kid at all costs."

The film relies on the nonlinearity of time and of film itself to undercut the conventional tragedy enacted in the house. Time never passes as we might expect: for example, Julie and a co-worker lay out Tarot cards for fortune-telling: "Your future is in the past," Julie is told, to which she responds, "So my future is in the present." As with many of Rivette's films, *Céline and Julie* mixes the experience of everyday, film, and theatrical time; running for more than three hours, it also challenges the spectator's expectations of viewing time, for it seems to never end. The women inhabit a languorous and open-ended "present time" in their apartment and the

Paris streets and parks; the "past time" in the house seems tighter, constituted in fragments that strain to cohere into a story. The film frequently inserts silent-film-like title cards between scenes labeled "Mais, le lendemain matin" ("But, the next morning"), suggesting both the "tomorrow and tomorrow and tomorrow" of everyday life and the repetition of tragic tales. As Julie Levinson comments on the story's temporality, "Céline pronounces this penny-dreadful plot a grand tragedy that smells like mothballs; she complains that it is 'toujours le même'" (242).[15]

Although Céline and Julie begin as passive participants in as well as spectators of the tragedy, when they finally enter the house together to save Madlyn they become comic actors and improvising performers, drawing on the implicit power of performance to transform a "script." We know that Juliet Berto and Dominique Labourier (who play Céline and Julie) composed the scenes outside of the tragic house through improvisation; in contrast, Eduardo De Gregorio wrote the text for the stilted and formal actions based on the two James stories. Once Céline and Julie enter into the house, the two styles obviously clash. Then the tragic drama disintegrates, where the change is signaled by the insertion of live theater in the film: a knocking evoking a play's opening in the French theater introduces the action, and at another moment applause awards Julie's "performance." When Céline and Julie insert themselves into the story, taking turns actively playing Miss Angèle, they first flub their lines and their entrances, not perfectly replicating what we would see as the "original" script. When they realize that the other characters will not react, they ramp up their clowning with the adults whose own lines and movements never change.

Céline and Julie are thus conscious that they are performing in two kinds of plots, comic and tragic, improvised and scripted, but their acting now has "real" consequences, for they are able to bring Madlyn from the house into the "real" world. When they go boating in the park, they encounter the three adults from the house standing frozen on another boat drifting in the opposite direction, perhaps a version of Rosencrantz's and Guildenstern's darker vision of life on a boat as movement "contained within a larger one that carries us along as inexorably as the wind and current" (122). But Céline and Julie's boating is something different: the title puns on what "aller en bateau" can mean in French—"to be taken for a ride, to be told a shaggy dog story" (Romney). Thus, for them, being on a boat means being unconfined by any known pathway, including marriage (since Céline breaks up Julie's engagement) and subjection to men (as Julie rescues Céline from her job as a nightclub performer). As Robin Wood comments, Céline and Julie are thus "marked as 'free,' able to invent their own lives; the 'house' characters are imprisoned in a predetermined performance, their lines given them by an author, their attitudes and actions determined by the dominant ideological assumptions [...] This is underlined by the repetition of lines, gestures, scenes: they are actors trapped in a perpetually repeated play [...]" (8). *Céline and Julie Go Boating* thus shows how, through the intrusion of a performative present into the past, unlike the male time travelers who must sacrifice themselves, the female travelers can seize temporal authority.

Rivette's appropriation of theatrical play and performance to undo tragic necessity also reflects the film's overall framework of a game. In describing their invention of Céline and Julie, Labourier has commented that "very often we tend to forget that the profession of an actress is, above all, based on games, like children's games. So in *Céline and Julie* [...] we started off with the notion of amusing ourselves by creating interchangeable characters in many different forms, in the style of a game" (Dasgupta). Games recur throughout the film: for example, the women playing with Tarot cards in Julie's library, or the game in which Madlyn must choose in which of Sophie's hands she will find a piece of candy. These clues draw attention to the film's playful frame, beginning with Julie's pursuing Céline through the Paris streets, and ending with Céline's pursuing Julie. After her rescue, Madlyn asks delightedly, "What game shall we play," and Céline responds, "No more playing ever." But she is wrong, since as the film ends, it is clear that the two women are in fact playing a game that begins again—and again. Unlike the deadly repetition of the tragic story in the house, however, their redoing always allows for difference.

As I suggested in the previous chapter considering drama and performance, a game structure allows for variation and freedom of choice within its rules. It also implies repeatability without linearity; the point of a game is that it can be played over and over, each time with a different possible outcome. As they start to enter the house together, Céline begins to chant, "Il était une fois" ("once upon a time") but Julie corrects her with "Il était deux fois...il était trois fois" (more like, "twice upon a time," or "two times," "three times"). Céline concludes that, "Il était que cette fois ce ne se passera pas comme ça—pas comme toutes les autres fois" ("it was that this time it will not happen like all the other times"). With its lack of grammatical sense and confusion of tense, this line expresses the essence of the film's twisting of time, which disrupts language itself. Their exchange also connects the story both to fairy-tale narrative conventions and to games, where if first you do not succeed, you can "try, try again."[16] Because of this fundamental disruption of the conventional operation of time, choice in time here becomes not catastrophic but rather part of a process rife with present opportunities.

When Tom Tykwer created his film of a female protagonist who manipulates time in a rescue scheme, he also turned to ideas of gaming and play to create a structure for reversing tragic choice and consequences. *Run Lola Run* begins with an epigraph from the German football coach S. Herberger: "Nach dem Spiel ist vor dem Spiel" ("After the game is before the game"), and the pronouncement, "The ball is round. The game lasts 90 minutes. That's a fact. Everything else is pure theory." In a review of the film, following this signal, Tom Whalen has argued that "the film's unifying principle is the Game": that is, it is like a game because it is "time-bound," it can be repeated, and "the player should be able to affect the outcome of the game." He concludes that in that sense *Run Lola Run* exists "in a zone of safety" because no one dies (33–4), but in fact, someone does die—twice. For the game to mean something, death must be possible where tragic temporality confronts "game thinking."

Run Lola Run presents three versions of a repeated 20-minute scenario, closely approximating the viewing time, in which Lola must come up with 100,000 marks to save her boyfriend Manni, who has lost money he owes to his petty crime boss. Initially Lola comes too late to save Manni from starting a supermarket hold-up for the cash, and she ends up being shot instead. But as she dies, she wills herself back to life, and the story begins again. When, in the second episode, Lola succeeds in getting the money herself by holding up her father's bank, Manni is hit by an ambulance. This time it is not a question of her being too late, but rather people being at the wrong place at the wrong time in a world fraught with accidents. Once again, Lola wills the scenario to repeat, and in the third version, she has apparently learned how to save her man (or Manni), and to make the right choices at critical moments: for example, to avoid a vicious dog on her apartment stairs or to hitch a ride rather than running. The film thus implies that the first and second versions of the twenty minutes are interconnected, and the repetition of the events amplifies Lola's power. She makes split-second strategic decisions that influence outcomes both for herself and for many others, as indicated in the rapid flashes of snapshots of the lives of those she touches, however briefly, in her three journeys across Berlin (also see Whalen, 36–7).

Several commentators have noted that *Run Lola Run* resembles a video-game, a form of play that tells a story but allows for rehearsing events (see Evans). Michael Wedel sees the resemblance in the film's style: for example, the animated title sequence reflects a perspective of a first-person shooter videogame (131–2). However, the most significant resemblance lies in Lola's three lives; like a videogame avatar, her life and Manni's can be reset when they die or fail. In *Run Lola Run* the cinematic time-loop mechanism, whereby the protagonist learns to solve a problem and produce a satisfactory outcome in a repeated present thus overlaps with the videogame's digital modality. The film thus develops the "game-like" base of the time-loop mode, which allows choice and free play within fixed parameters.

Both *Run Lola Run* and *Céline and Julie Go Boating* thus construct a feminist platform in which the protagonist can seize control of present time, drawing a tragic drama into a game. The effects reflect the tension of participatory theater as explored in Chap. 2, in which a story defined by its past shape breaks up when converted into a present event—but in these films, the protagonists also *own* the present. My previous chapters have emphasized uncovering the conditions of productive uncertainty embedded in tragic drama: how can we see beyond the anxiety of acting in that onrushing present to recognize all that the present makes possible? By looking at how many time-travel films represent resistance to tragic temporality through the protagonist's struggle to control the means of time and defy authority, this chapter has focused in turn on what might happen under conditions of uncertainty by grappling directly with questions of agency or action in present versus past time. Most films still depict agents locked into the screen's story, thus separating the spectators from the action and denying them the opportunity to do anything other than follow the scenes that flicker before them. However, *Céline and Julie*, before its time, and *Run Lola Run*, of its time, anticipate a different kind of enacted story, a narrative in which the spectator becomes the actor and the director, seizing the camera that stands in for the present time. For that, we must turn to this book's final chapter.

NOTES

1. On time-travel films and "undoing," see Gallagher, who suggests that this "enlarged sense of temporal possibility correlates with a newly activist, even interventionist, relation to our collective past" (12) (Gallagher 2002).

2. See Wachhorst: "The fundamental components of the time-travel romance are (1) a male time traveler who encounters (2) a female inhabitant of another time" (341) (Wachhorst 1984).

3. Penley notes how, in turn, in *The Terminator* and *Back to the Future Part 1*, traveling in time is connected with the "primal scene," where the object of desire also stands in for the mother. See also Wachhorst (1984).

4. Cardwell qualifies this point herself in stating that "the film image is not inherently present, it is inherently tenseless" (88) (Cardwell 2003).

5. See Deren on how cinematic time can be manipulated, slowed down, or reversed (149) (Deren 2011).

6. Wittenberg also argues that film is like a time travel, insofar as "time travel is already fundamentally a visual medium" (147) (Wittenberg 2013). See also Landon (71) (Landon 1992).

7. There are exceptions: for example, Terry Gilliam's *Time Bandits* needs no machine because it has religion; similarly, the replaying of time in *Run Lola Run* appears to happen solely through the force of Lola's will and her love for Manni.

8. See Wittenberg, who also notes that "we might consider time travel in film a multiplex surveillance of *fabular* lines, and therefore continuous with the thematic linking of film-viewing and surveillance technology that has pre-occupied mainstream cinema from Hitchcock's *Rear Window* through a recent spate of hyperbolic world-viewing fantasies such as *Déjà Vu, Enemy of the State, Source Code,* and *The Adjustment Bureau*" (199) (Wittenberg 2013).

9. See Del Rio on the omnipresent use of technology and surveillance in *12 Monkeys* (387–8) (Del Rio 2001). In that film video dominates the world of the past as well: a television screen plays in the mental hospital where Cole first finds himself; the televisions mostly play cartoons and movie clips that would be seen as coming from the "past" (e.g., the Marx Brothers movies and old time-travel cartoons) to the "present" of film's audience in 1995.

10. *Looper* begins with the voice of young Joe conjugating the French verb *avoir*, which can be both the present tense of the verb "to have" but also the beginning of the *passé composé*: he then offers the temporally contradictory statement: "Time travel has not yet been invented but 30 years from now it will have been."

11. See Bordwell on films with "forking paths" plots, including *Sliding Doors, Blind Chance, Run Lola Run,* and *Too Many Ways to be Number 1*. The plot of *Donnie Darko* depends on our understanding that there is a "primary universe" and a "tangent universe," created by an unexplained, accidental cosmic anomaly. See also Gallagher on what she calls "Y" plots. (Gallagher 2002)

12. The positing of alternate or parallel universes does often turn on the notion that a chance occurrence of a moment in time can set off a tangled chain of circumstances. In *Blind Chance*, catching a train—or not—triggers three different versions of a man's life. But in all of these cases, no moral choice or decision triggers the different narrative; it is just an accident of timing. *Sliding Doors* adapts the concept of *Blind Chance*: there the life of the protagonist Helen takes two paths, depending on whether or not she catches a train on the London underground railway. The two stories then run simultaneously, alternating between the two "universes"the one which appears to be the comic version ends suddenly and tragically, with her death; the other "dramatic" one ends with her survival and the implication of the happy ending.

13. See Matz, "Aesthetic/Prosthetic" on the ways in which *Source Code* also offers an idea of "prosthetic" time (Matz 2016).

14. In his introduction to the Criterion DVD, Jonathan Romney calls it a "time travel adventure."

15. On concepts of "women's time" in feminist theory, see Apter (2010)

16. In its exploration of games as a structure for narrative, *Céline and Julie* also echoes Jean Resnais's *Last Year At Marienbad*, which also radically distorts temporality, while playing out a potentially tragic love story. See Bordwell and Thompson on how the whole structure of *Marienbad* is "a play with logic, space, and time which does not offer us a single, complete story as a prize for winning this 'game.' [...] But *Marienbad* broke with conventional expectations by suggesting, perhaps for the first time in film history, that a narrative film could base itself entirely on a game-like structure of causal, spatial, and temporal ambiguity, refusing to specify explicit meanings and teasing the viewer with hints about elusive implicit meanings" (396) (Bordwell and Thompson 1992).

CHAPTER 4

Tragic Time and Choice in Videogames

Abstract This chapter argues that while engaging the player as spectator, actor, and author, videogames both draw on and revert back to the essential tensions inherent in the tragic experience of time. Through a discussion of serious narrative games such as *The Wolf Among Us, Heavy Rain, Mass Effect,* and *The Stanley Parable,* the chapter describes how games thrive through creating an environment of choice in which the player is constantly offered options of speech and action, and in this, a form of authorship to create both plot and character. While they may evoke the harrowing sensation familiar from tragedy of having to act in a crisis, yet they can also offer the player the chance to undo that decision by reversing time, revisiting the past in a new present, and then moving forward having learned what the future will bring. This replay may feel like asserting freedom from the "tyranny" of the story because one can repeat and remain in a present time when all things seem possible and under the player's control. However, one cannot forget that the player is operating within the context of the program, limited by the choices offered and the game's intent. The chapter ends by considering the role of cheating and modding in the disruption of game plotting.

Keywords Time · Temporality · Choice · Crisis · Tragedy · Drama · Fate · Videogames · Play · Games · Cheating · Modding · Interactivity · *The Wolf Among Us* · *Heavy Rain* · *The Stanley Parable* · *Mass Effect* · *Life is Strange*

© The Author(s) 2016
R. Bushnell, *Tragic Time in Drama, Film, and Videogames,*
DOI 10.1057/978-1-137-58526-4_4

Given the examples of temporal game-play in *Céline and Julie Go Boating* and *Run Lola Run*, the time has come for this book to end where it began, with the proposition that in their experimentation with the play of choice and consequences, videogames have something to teach us about the deep structure of tragedy. In the past two decades, more scholars have been taking videogames seriously, both as a form of art and theater and as a medium outpacing movies in terms of popularity.[1] Readers unfamiliar with videogames or who think of them only as mindless entertainment might protest against their inclusion in a book like this one. But increasingly people are fashioning games with strong narratives that involve serious questions of moral responsibility. A videogame can be ethically complex, leading many advocates to argue that "videogames matter" (the subtitle of Tom Bissell's *Extra Lives*).

In these games, the player is simultaneously a playwright, a director, a character, an actor bringing the character to life, and a spectator who observes the action unfolding. The player controls the actions of an avatar from either a first-person or a third-person camera view and thus produces a kind of theatrical performance. Videogames may lack live bodies to enact the story, but they are like theater insofar as they are stories enacted by virtual moving bodies, responding to the player's commands and interacting with the game environment in present time.[2] Because they involve graphical movement (mostly in three dimensions), these games are not texts, although they work like written hypertexts in their narrative branching. They may look like films at times, but they differ significantly from films because they are interactive—they are truly *games*, and the gameplay is central to their function. Some critics might want to argue that this interactivity would strictly differentiate videogames from theater as well as film, which more formally separate the functions of author, actor, character, and audience. But, as I have suggested in Chap. 2, theatrical performance can also blur those boundaries, and videogames just take this to the next stage. Their hybrid nature as both narratives and games, or what some have called "ludonarratives" (see Bissell 36–38), naturally generates the kind of conflict found in participatory theater between "narrative power and the tensions of a sporting match" (Schechner, *Performance Theory* 53).

In Chap. 2, I argued that even though a tragic play may be "scripted," each theatrical performance in fact can be considered temporally unique and thus potentially contingent. Like most plays, videogames are also scripted insofar as they are highly complex programs, not random assemblages of data. However, because they are meant to be games before anything else, videogames embed multiple versions that can unfold as a result of the player's actions, and each iteration of the game may substantially differ from the next one. In some games, those choices are only "modular" (*Performance Theory* 53), affecting the process of playing, while the story will always end the same way. In other games, however, the player's actions can significantly change the outcome. Further, in the tragic theater, once a choice is made, it seems irrevocable; in contrast, in a videogame, if the player errs, whether through a poor decision or mere ineptness, sometimes he or she may try again, knowing what the future brings. Like the time-travel films discussed in Chap. 3, videogames thus challenge assumptions about how present choices can both shape character and construct plot. By experiencing a repeated present time, the player can see clearly how these actions, whether deliberate or rash, set the course to a particular end. When the program permits or invites it, videogames may thus satisfy that desire to control the progression of time, providing what Paul Booth has described as "the complex pleasures of meaningful participation in one's own temporal existence" (140). In so doing they expose the working of the machine of necessity, reminding us that in the theater and in games, the end is never really the end.

While I could discuss many games, a few will serve as core "texts" for this chapter, because they so explicitly involve questions of significant choice, character, and consequences. In particular, Tell-Tale Games' *The Wolf Among Us* is a fascinating detective story that crosses fairy tales with film noir. It is enacted in a half-real, half-fantasy world called Fabletown, mapped onto a decaying but recognizable New York City inhabited by people who can morph into fabled monsters and animals who can talk. In this game world Bigby the sheriff (identified in the "fable" fiction with the "Big Bad Wolf") pursues a serial killer. The player guides Bigby through the story, having conversations, studying clues, interrogating witnesses, and getting into fights. While seeking justice in this dysfunctional society of misfits, Bigby grapples with his own violent or literally wolf-like nature. The choices the player makes may not significantly influence the narrative's outcome but they do shape Bigby's moral character and how others treat him.

Like *The Wolf Among Us*, the hyper-realistic *Heavy Rain* follows four characters in a search for a serial killer of children named the Origami Killer. In order to save his son Shaun, whom the serial killer has kidnapped, the story's central character Ethan Mars has to endure many trials, including driving the wrong way down a highway, climbing through a tunnel of broken glass, cutting off his own finger, and killing a man. The player also acts through three other characters: a journalist, a FBI profiler, and a private detective, all engaged in the search, and one of whom turns out to be the serial killer himself. In this extremely anxiety-filled game, the actions the player chooses for all four avatars can lead to eighteen possible endings, ranging from a happy one in which justice is served to a catastrophic one in which all four main characters die.

VIDEOGAME TIME

Even more than in theatrical performance and film, the temporality of videogames is both volatile and multi-layered.[3] In writing about performative time in games, theater, and sports, Richard Schechner has observed that "orthodox theater" mostly sticks to what he calls "symbolic time," a play time representing another kind of clock time, but unrelated to the actual time of the performance itself. In contrast, experimental theater may also use "event time," a time like that of baseball, in which the players must complete all the steps of the game no matter how long it takes. Some performances (and many sports) may also use "set time," in which players fight the clock to complete certain tasks or overcome an opponent (*Performance Theory* 8–10). (Of course, orthodox theater also employs "set time" insofar as the performance length may be limited to what the prologue to *Romeo and Juliet* calls the "two hours' traffic of [the] stage.") As "performances" videogames mostly replicate the mixed temporality of experimental theater, using symbolic, event, and set time, where symbolic time is the time of the story told (as hours, days, or years), event time is the time of the playing of the game itself (which could be minutes, hours, or days), and set time, the often extremely limited amount of time a player might have to complete a given task or action.[4] Many videogames also employ "cut scenes," cinematic interludes that advance the story while the player can only watch.[5]

Often videogame time goes very slowly and feels totally in the player's control, when an avatar explores a new space or environment, simulating the experience of everyday time. Such temporality is typical of games which encourage the player to explore the environment by conversing with other characters, examining things, reading messages, and doing things germane to advancing the plot. *Heavy Rain* uses this strategy to make the player complete more or less mundane tasks such as making lunch, reading mail, and feeding a baby before the game can proceed, creating a sense of present, lived time.[6] Many games may take dozens of hours to finish, depending on the player's skill or style; some like to wander, experiencing the entire game environment, while others like to plunge ahead to the action. Whatever her choices, the player controls the pace.

Sometimes, however, the player cannot ignore time's passing as marked by a ticking clock or countdown, a "set time" in which she has a strictly limited period to accomplish a task or beat an opponent.[7] Running against *Heavy Rain's* leisurely domestic temporality is the constant flow of rain that falls during the search for the kidnapped child. The serial killer sends the message that Shaun will die when six inches of rain have fallen, and the game keeps track of its accumulation. So while the actual pace of playing the game can be slow, the player still senses that she is under time pressure. The game's designer David Cage has claimed that he did this because the rain was something "that no one can stop, no one has any control over. That it would be a countdown" (Ohannessian).

This set time speeds up further and appears completely out of the player's control when she encounters a "quick time event" and must act immediately, whether in dialogue or deadly conflict. Such moments generate the acute sense of a present time that cannot be stopped that has been seen as characteristic of tragic temporality, as opposed to everyday, lived time.[8] Jesper Juul describes such moments as an intense "sense of happening *now* when you play. Pressing a key [or a button] influences the game world, which then logically and intuitively has to be happening in the same *now*" (Juul, "The Game" 132). Typically, the player then confronts significant decisions, with only seconds to act before the game chooses instead. In some cases, the alternatives are inconsequential, but in others they are critical and even life-threatening. To survive such an encounter, without time to think the player often just resorts to reflexes. *Heavy Rain* makes choosing even more difficult by having the text options for actions dance around the screen and fade in and out. Once when I was controlling the game's FBI profiler Norman Jayden, he was interrogating Nathan, a religious fanatic suspected of the crimes. When Nathan pulled a gun on Jayden I was given a dizzying set of alternatives: should I have Jayden shoot him or talk him down? In a panic, I pushed the wrong button, and through my mistake Jayden killed Nathan. If, as Charles Bernstein has observed, "controlled anxiety is one of the primary 'hooks' into the medium" (163), here the anxiety was so intense that it practically unhinged me.[9]

Of course, sometimes a game may ease the panic of such events by offering the chance to replay them, that is, to turn back time. Jesper Juul has noted the irony that "this is what games do: they promise us that we can repair a personal inadequacy—an inadequacy they produce in us in the first place" (*Art of Failure* 7). Games typically have a "save" function (either automatic or manual) whereby the player can return to a "checkpoint" and redo the action from that point in the story. Sometimes that opportunity comes when an avatar dies in combat and that character must survive in order for the game to proceed.[10] As in the time-loop films discussed in Chap. 3, here mistakes can be permanently erased, when the player learns from experience. As Chuck Moran has described what he calls these "undoings," "in the relaxed time made available by undo commands, configuration is privileged over performance, death is deferrable, interruption minimized, precision trained, urgency optional, uncertainty resolved, and some of games' harsh discipline sidestepped" ("Playing with Game Time").

In many cases, however, the player cannot go back: the program determines that. *Heavy Rain* also did not give me a chance to undo the unintended shooting of Nathan. Further, that game does not let any of the main characters die until the final episode, but when they do die then as a result of the player's actions, there is no replay. Only when you finish *Heavy Rain* can you go back to repeat given episodes to see how things might have turned out differently. In an early scene in *The Wolf Among Us*, Sheriff Bigby has to fight a troll engagingly named Grendel. Because of my incompetence with the controller, when I played the game Bigby died multiple times, but each time the game did automatically reset to let me try again. So Bigby died and died again until I learned how to defeat his antagonist. However, once Bigby finally overcame Grendel, I had to choose quickly between Bigby's tearing off the troll's arm or letting him go. In fear and frustration, I opted to tear off Grendel's arm, and I was not permitted to reverse that decision. For the rest of the game Grendel held that aggression against Bigby, and that became part of the Fabletown community's emotional response to Bigby's character.

Many videogames have made turning back time a theme of the game itself.[11] At the time of my writing this chapter, Wikipedia listed dozens of video games with time travel as part of the story line or as an element of gameplay in them.[12] For example, the *Super-Mario-Brothers*-like puzzle game *Braid* tells the player at first that the protagonist Tim is on a quest to rescue a princess and to right an unspecified wrong ("Tim," it is said, "made a mistake"). Each of the game's six levels offers a different way of manipulating gameplay time. While the player needs to move Tim from left to right, imitating the forward flow of time, he or she may also move

Tim backward, reversing time to repeat an action. As reviewer Dan Whitehead has described the process, the player must "embrace the idea that you can set things up in the future before rewinding to the past for the payoff" ("Braid"). The ironies of the gameplay extend to the story itself. In the game's conclusion, when the action is played backward, it appears in reverse that, rather than Tim pursuing the princess to save her, she is running *away* from him: he is a villain, not a hero.

Of course, this kind of game only permits the player to manipulate time in order to learn to do what the game demands, or in Mark Wolf's words, to "give the correct response or perform the correct action" (*Medium* 81). In games like *Braid*, in the end, choice is not really an option, since to proceed one must complete a set of actions in the right order and thus solve a puzzle. In games that involve serious moral choices, however, more is at stake. For example, in *Life is Strange* Maxine Caufield, a boarding school student, must deal with a mystery concerning another student's disappearance as well as her prophetic vision of a future superstorm. Much of the game action concerns Max's involvement with her friends' lives as she seeks answers to questions about both past and future. At significant points Max (i.e., the player) can rewind time to see what the consequences of certain dialogue or action decisions might be. *Life is Strange* thus explicitly connects the mechanics of replay with time travel, where information learned from multiple attempts can be used to solve a problem or to review a moral choice based on what the game shows as the immediate consequences (while it leaves the player in the dark about the longer-term effects).[13]

So what really is a "correct action" in a game like this? Sometimes the "correct action" can be unambiguous—opening the right door or picking up a clue—but often it is not always clear what is right, when a game is ethically complex. In the same way that Gary Saul Morson is concerned about the positing of multiple universes, Miguel Sicart worries that too much rewinding of time in gameplay *reduces* a game's potential ethical impact. He believes a game should pose what he calls a "wicked problem," one with no clear-cut "correct action." He asks:

How can a consequence be important if players can reload and return to the state where decisions are still possible? If ethical gameplay is personal, then play is not safe, and we cannot explore through play with no consequences. For play to matter personally, safety needs to be reduced, and emotional opening for interpretation need to be increased. (101–102)[14]

Every complex game narrative thus has to find the right balance between reducing frustration and anxiety so that the player can continue playing and retain an emotional investment in decisions that matter.

Further, it is not always clear when a player makes a choice in the present what the impact will be.[15] While *Life is Strange* allows for reversing time, the player can only see the short-term outcome of a decision. As the game's designer Jean-Maxime Moris has said:

> None of the choices in *Life is Strange* are clear cut. [...] You can always rewind and do things differently, which is going to have repercussions down the line. Some of those repercussions are short-term, some of those are medium-term and some of those are long-term. And for each one of your choices that you make there's no definite answer. Something good in the short-term might turn out worse later. (Purchese)

Similarly, in *Heavy Rain* the player constantly confronts moral or emotional decisions as well as physical trials without knowing in advance what they will eventually mean. For example, Ethan Mars faces a critical choice when he must accept or reject the love of Madison, the journalist who helps him when he is on the run from the police. He is angry because he has just discovered she is a journalist, and he suspects that she has only befriended him to write a story about him. The player's decision at this moment will affect the ending, but at this point she can only guess how (she would later find out that if both Ethan and Madison as well as Shaun survive at the end, and if Ethan has accepted Madison at this point, they will marry; if Shaun dies, Ethan will always commit suicide, but his acceptance or rejection of Madison will trigger several different ways of ending his and her stories).

Choice and Character

One of the most important interventions a player makes in a game is constructing her avatar character, which can have important consequences in the game's outcome. In most cases, videogames start with an avatar having a basic profile and backstory, but part of the point of the game is to develop that character through his or her interactions. So, for example, in *The Wolf Among Us*, the player begins with Bigby as a rough but relatively neutral creature, but soon even minor decisions can shape the evolution of Bigby's character as a violent enforcer of justice or as rational negotiator.

When trying to "be" Bigby, I took the non-violent route whenever I could, except when I had to defend Bigby from attack, and I had no alternative. Sometimes when choosing between a diplomatic or violent response to a threat or situation, the player cannot tell if the game can progress without Bigby's becoming more aggressive. What one does choose will later affect how the other characters present at the encounter interact with Bigby for the rest of the game (the game often informs the player that this or that character will "remember that").[16] While individual choices do not change the overall outcome of the story (Bigby must overcome the Crooked Man for the game to end), the cumulative power of all these choices surfaces when the game's characters all come together as a community to consider how to punish the Crooked Man: will they attempt some sort of judgment by the rule of law, or will it be done in the spirit of mob violence and revenge?

Perhaps the most complicated scheme for the development of game character that I have seen occurs in *Mass Effect*, a massive sci-fi adventure role-playing trilogy centered on Commander Shepard, who undertakes a mission to save the galaxy from a race of beings called the Reapers. Shepard is both the leader of a team and a fighter who does a lot of killing of aliens along the way.[17] The player begins by constructing Shepard's gender and appearance as well as his or her origin ("spacer," "earthborn," or "colonist"), military class, and programmed psychological profile ("sole survivor," "war hero," or "ruthless"). As *Mass Effect* proceeds, through interaction with non-player-controlled (or NPC) characters, the player further shapes Shepard's character as a "paragon" or a "renegade," the game's basic moral parameters. As Hilary Goldstein and Erik Brudvig have described it: "your actions will reward you with points that accumulate on a moral compass of sorts. The paragon meter fills with just and honorable actions. Renegade players will look for the easy and fast way out of any situation, regardless of how many toes get stepped on or chopped off" ("Paragon and Renegade"). Selections of action and dialogue are made from a graphic "wheel," where the player knows by the option's wheel position what the game designers have decided a paragon or a renegade would say or do (paragon responses on the upper right, renegade responses on the lower right). Thus the player does not necessarily have to intuit what a paragon or renegade would say; instead, in what amounts to an exercise in moral education, the game indicates that this is how such a person would act or speak.[18] As the player continues, his or her choices "unlock" more paragon or renegade options, depending on what has been chosen before.[19]

Some game choices made in *Mass Effect* are strategic, having either or short or long-term effect on the actions, while others function more to shape Shepard's character and thus his or her relationships with the other characters, but all are in one way or another consequential. For example, some decisions can either strengthen or weaken the team's loyalty to Shepard, ultimately affecting who might survive at the end. In contrast to the choices made in *The Wolf Among Us*, here building character really matters for the shape of the story itself. While in *Mass Effect* at certain points one can replay choices or actions, because of its length and complexity the game makes it very difficult to do so, and thus, as in *Heavy Rain*, the player must live with the consequences of her decisions.

Such structures for character construction found in *A Wolf Among Us* and *Mass Effect* do imply a deliberative process at work, but, as my tearing off of Grendel's arm indicates, a player can easily lose control of a situation and react emotionally. When I had Bigby tear off Grendel's arm rather than letting him go, it was certainly not a rational decision; to my surprise, in that instant, the "wolf" in me, and thus the wolf in Bigby (the "Big Bad Wolf") came out. Because of time pressure and the stress of acting in the moment, the player's relative level of game-play skill can thus shape choice. The player may struggle in navigating the virtual world, when hitting the computer keys or pressing the controller buttons *now* translate into physical actions.[20] Jonathan McCalmont has reflected on the implications of his own incompetence for the construction of Ethan's character in *Heavy Rain*:

> By giving us characters that all share a certain degree of hollowness and then allowing us complete responsibility for their destinies, *Heavy Rain* allows us to create identities for each of these four characters. For example, as I am shockingly bad at quick time events and played the game on a low-resolution TV, I frequently struggled to a) make it through the quick time events unscathed and b) make the dialogue selections that seemed most reasonable to me. As a result of my cack-handedness, Ethan Mars rapidly turned into a shambling wreck, a borderline-psychotic ruin of a man who had nothing to live for except the chance that he might save his son from a serial killer. As this character emerged from my own incompetence, my vision of Mars began to shape my decisions: he did not hesitate to maim himself; he took insane risks when confronted by the police; he gleefully crawled across glass; he drank poison. Nothing mattered to him except Shaun." ("Free Will").

Like my own, McCalmont's experience shows how the player cannot so easily map his or her own character onto that of the avatar.[21] James Paul Gee has labeled what happens between game player and avatar a case of "projective identity," when one both projects "one's values and desires onto the virtual character" and makes the character a "project" (Gee 2014, 55), but the relationship is an unstable one, dependent on a player's relative ability to make a character do what she wants.[22]

Other factors besides the player's skill level can influence the construction of a character, creating a gap between player and avatar. Sometimes the player seems to have no choice, if the story is to go on: one must fight, because that is either what the game designers think the player wants, or what such a story demands. The player may also *not* want to have an avatar mirror herself, instead experimenting with another identity or seeing what it feels like to be an assassin or a renegade. Mawhorter et al. discuss how players can bring different motivations to a game and how their choices may diverge according to those distinct motives, including ones that are "diegetic" (e.g., achieving a goal), "semi-diegetic" (e.g., sympathy for a character), and "extradiegetic" (e.g., playing for an audience) (3). Further, many games provide incentive for actions that do not necessarily have to do with the story: for example, *Heavy Rain* awards the player "trophies" for having completed certain tasks, where awards become an end in themselves, irrelevant to any moral considerations.

In videogames the construction of character in the present of playing emerges in "real time" from the interaction of the player's "projective identity" and performance with the game's inherent structure of incentives and demands. While the avatar's character may first be mapped according to the player's values and physical and mental abilities, that character may also take on a life of its own (see Gee Chap. 3). When the player makes choices at critical moments, they are free in one sense while still constrained by the options the game offers. In turn, those choices can redound by routing the action for the game's future, as, for example, in *Mass Effect*, where paragon or renegade choices affect the dialogue and action options the player is offered later, when the game responds over time.

When the player thus participates in a process in which character explicitly emerges from present decision-making process, videogames expose the mechanism of constructing dramatic character through choice in time as explored in Chap. 1. The player experiences what it means to act in a present that is both in and out of her control: sometimes it is a slow unfolding present that allows for deliberation, and sometimes it is terrifyingly fast, making the player act in the panic of the moment when the game cannot be paused. Once choices have been made, whether rashly or rationally, if the move cannot be replayed, the program then responds by channeling the character and sometimes the action in one direction. Yet at other times, when a replay is allowed and the past repeated in the present, games can offer the player insight into how choice shapes character. Because of this dynamic interaction of player and game in time, videogames complicate the very notion of choice: is the player indeed free in the game, or does the game ultimately play her?

CHOICE AND CONSEQUENCES

By offering the player a form of agency through choice, videogames thus seem to endow her with responsibility for the outcome or the "fate" of the characters. Many game critics have written quite powerfully of how playing these games feels like a "full-body experience" (Bissell 126) when players enter the lives of their avatars and then witness the consequences.[23] In Bissell's words:

> Games such as *Mass Effect* allow the gamer a freedom of decision that can be evilly enlivening or nobly self-congratulating, but these games become uniquely compelling when they force you to the edge of some drawn, real-life line of intellectual or moral obligation that, to your mild astonishment, you find you cannot step across even in what is, essentially, a digital dollhouse for adults. Other mediums may depict the necessary (or foolhardy) breaches of such lines, or their foolhardy (or necessary) protection, but only games actually push you to the line's edge and make you live with the fictional consequences of your choice. (24)

In *Heavy Rain*, after failing two trials and succeeding in only one (cutting off Ethan's finger, which was excruciatingly hard to do), I had to stop playing the game because it was causing me so much anxiety. Further, because I was reading the extensive on-line walk-through guide on the *Heavy Rain* wikis, I knew what all the possible endings were.[24] Because of my foreknowledge of the plot, I came to realize because of my previous mistakes, I was unlikely to be able to save Ethan's son and create any ending but one in which Ethan commits suicide (it is possible for other characters to save Shaun, but they too must survive many contests to reach the end). I thus reached the breaking point that both the audience and actors in *Dionysus in 69* once reached: you could say I walked out of the theater and read the book instead, because I could not bear the responsibility for a tragic ending.

Of course, in many videogames, the death which so many people identify with the end of tragedy is not always death, when a "game over" only means a reset (just as in the cinematic time-loop frameworks of *Source Code* or *Edge of Tomorrow: Live Die Repeat*). Even in *Heavy Rain*, after the player finishes the game, she can go back and replay certain episodes, which will then change the outcome for the various characters.[25] David Cage has taken two different positions on how this ability to redo the episodes relates to "life itself." In an interview in 2009, Cage insisted he "would like people to play [the game] once [...] because that's life. Life you can only play once [...] I would like people to have this experience that way" (Gaskill).[26] But in 2010 he said instead, "I really enjoy the idea that there is *not one story* [...] I like the fact that there are many possibilities, because I think this is what life is about. [...] *Heavy Rain* is very close to real life, much more than a movie where you can only know one possibility. In *Heavy Rain* you really feel like you have the choice, and what happens to you depends on you" (Ohannessian). Inherent in Cage's two statements is a confusion of game, art, and "real life." On the one hand, the conventional idea of the linear experience of tragic time is identified with "reality," but then, on the other hand, what is "real" is instead felt to be the experience of choice in present time and the idea of multiple possibilities latent in folded time.

Jesper Juul suggests that "we probably do not feel entirely responsible for tragic events in a game since they are neither real nor entirely within our control. After all, for any linear game, it is the game designer who designed the suffering and made it unavoidable" (*Art of Failure* 112–3).[27] If this is so, playing a game should be like the experience of a tragic spectator who knows what is to come and not implicitly granted the power to do anything about it; the spectators have paid to see the play, the actors have prepared, and the show must work itself to a conclusion. But games are different insofar as we enter into the game with the expectation that our actions can make a difference for the outcome. For example, the first episode of *Heavy Rain* ends with a scene in which Ethan Mars' family visits a mall. Ethan, controlled by the player, is supposed to be looking after his younger son Jason, who suddenly disappears. The game then subjects the player to a panicked search for Jason in a crowd. Whether or not the player finds Jason

(I never did), the game moves outside to a cut scene in which, despite Ethan's efforts, Jason is killed by a car. I was first racked with guilt thinking that my—or Ethan's—failure to find Jason must have caused his death. I then realized that to set up the plot, Jason had to die, whether he was found or not. In videogames, precisely because one has been given the chance to participate and act, such moments depriving one of the power to act are even more devastating.

Some videogames could thus be said to offer the contradictions of a "life on a boat" as described in *Rosencrantz and Guildenstern Are Dead*: while Guildenstern cheerfully suggests that here they can do "what we like and say what we like to whomever we like, without restriction," Rosencrantz responds, "Within limits, of course" (116). Such is the effect of a game like *The Wolf Among Us*, in which the outcome is always the same while the characterization may vary, or in *Heavy Rain* played only one way through. In another game, *Bioshock Infinite*, the player's avatar is Booker Dewitt, given the mission to rescue a woman called Elizabeth trapped in the floating city of Columbia, a fantasy world ruled by a powerful white supremacist. It is said that Elizabeth has the power to create "tears" in the space–time continuum, and indeed throughout the game the story leads the players and Elizabeth into different moments in time. But the game does not provide the player with consequential choices.[28] The game's characters describe its world as one of "constants and variables," but the story will always end in the same place and way. In this world of "constants and variables" you "swim in different oceans and land on the same shore" (quoted in Phillips).

This is the moment to return to *The Stanley Parable*, the game with which this book began, remembering its parody of all the contradictions inherent in both gaming and tragic choice. As one reviewer of the game, Christian Donlan, puts it:

> *The Stanley Parable* is a video game that plays you. It examines questions of control and free will within a finite interactive space and asks: can you truly express yourself in a world in which an omniscient designer has already carved out all of your possibilities in advance? Is there real victory to be won inside a machine that has been pre-programmed to deliver victory to you anyway? ("The Stanley Parable Review")

The Stanley Parable, in short, is a game about choice and consequences made in present time, in the act of playing, and in a play that is a program.

Seen in retrospect, it evokes the ludic contest in *Hamlet* between Hamlet and his own story, where it appears that the only way to appear "free" is to "let be," choosing not to choose. As *The Stanley Parable* concludes in the "freedom" ending, the narrator tells us that when he left the office building with many puzzles still unsolved, Stanley recognized that "it was not knowledge that he was seeking, or even power, but happiness": "perhaps his goal had not been to understand, but to let go."

But not all gamers are content to remain within the parameters of the program. Over the history of videogaming, many player communities have learned to find and create tools to override the game worlds' programs. Cheating is rampant in videogames, not just underground but also openly, when player use internal or external cheat codes to get around the explicit game rules, for example to shoot straighter or grant a character infinite life (see Gee Chap. 7). Sometimes game designers hide cheat codes in the program itself, allowing them to be "unlocked" by a certain sequence of actions; for designers they provide a way to speed through a game, but players can find and share them. Such tools might seem like just another level of control, merely drawing the player into a deeper level of the program with an illusion of power or authorship, but they also pose a conflict between player and designer when the program punishes the gamer for cheating.[29]

More controversial is the effect of "modding," or modification of games and programs that can change everything, a practice that generates the kinds of resistance and pleasure commonly associated with the forms of theatrical adaptation discussed in Chap. 2. In modding, fans can legally or illegally change games they play with changes ranging from simple add-ons or patches to total rewrites (see Galloway on modding in relationship to avant garde cinema; Bogost on modding that is encouraged by developers; Meades on illegal modding). Modding participates in the broader game phenomenon called "counterplay": as Alan Meades defines it, counterplay is an often ugly "form of play defined by its working against a rule, against consensus, against etiquette, or against law" (1).[30] In counterplay, players resist the assumption that the only right or successful way to play is to cooperate with the program. For example, when the final part of the *Mass Effect* trilogy was first released, many players criticized the game's ending, because they felt that the final choices given were too constrained and not sufficiently connected to the choices they had made earlier. In response to this player outrage, the game's designers released an alternative ending, which lowered the bar for the level of achievement needed to unlock all the possible endings and provided a fourth ambiguous conclusion. For those still not satisfied, one gamer independently created out of parts of the existing game the "Mass Effect Happy Ending Mod" in which Shepard lives and is reunited with his or her crew. While theatrical adaptation can translate a story in another version or medium, modding thus allows for a story to be disrupted at its very roots, a form of transgression which is, in Aarseth's words, "a symbolic gesture of rebellion against the tyranny of the game, a (perhaps illusory) way for the played subjects to regain their sense of identity and uniqueness through the mechanisms of the game itself" (132).

While engaging the player as spectator, actor, and author in that experience, videogames thus both draw on and revert back to the essential tensions inherent in the tragic experience of time. These games thrive through creating an environment of choice in which the player is constantly offered options of speech and action, and through these, a form of authorship: the power to create both plot and character. Games can indeed evoke the harrowing sensation, familiar from tragedy, of having to act in a panic, when confronted by a decision that may literally be a matter of life and death, yet they can also offer the player the chance to undo that decision by reversing time, revisiting the past in a new present, and then moving forward having learned what the future will bring. This replay may feel like asserting freedom from the "tyranny" of the story because one can repeat and remain in a present time when all things seem possible and under the player's control. At the same time, in so doing a gamer may be merely learning to follow the track of what the game requires her to do, to advance to another stage of the story that it has anticipated. The game wants you to play on, and for most of us, unless we have tools to break into the story at the level of its coding, the only way to become free of it is to put down the controls, turn off the machine, and walk away.[31] However, as Roger Caillois reminds us, "a game which one would be forced to play would at once cease to be play" (6): we can always be free of a game.

"THE END IS NEVER THE END IS NEVER THE END"

Chapter 1 began this book by introducing the idea of tragic time through Northrop Frye's evocation of an anxious present, "being in time, the sense of the one-directional quality of life, where everything happens once and for all, where every act brings unavoidable and fateful consequences, and where all experience vanishes, not simply into the past, but into nothingness, annihilation" (3). But since then I have argued that the alternative is to see the present as a time in process, like the temporality of participatory performance where meaning can be created freely. Videogames offer the experience of watching yourself acting in a suspended present, when the player is at once author, actor, character, and spectator, at moments (but not all moments) seizing control of time. Time-travel films fulfill the fantasy of watching the filmmaker turn back the traveler's time, but in videogames you experience that power yourself. In offering that power, the games offer both the emotional thrill of the constrained present but also a dynamic relationship to it. Through gaming, we come to understand better how time works in creating a story, because we make it and we live it.

At the end of *The Stanley Parable* the viewer encounters a screen in which the words "The End Is Never The End" are repeated, running across the page from left to right and top to bottom, only stopping when it meets the edge. Like the end of *Céline and Julie Go Boating*, in signaling its end the game simultaneously declares that it is not the end, for the game can always begin again. As Daniel Sack writes in the epilogue to *After Live*, "I would prefer not to end," (187) and I agree. Playing videogames has reminded me that from its beginnings in ancient Greece, tragedy's imposition of the end is one of its most powerful illusions. As I suggested in Chap. 1, the experience of tragedy is often defined by anticipating the end we both fear and crave: death and a conclusion that can be at once an imposition of judgment, a moment of ecstatic self-assertion, and an escape. But the centrality of repetition in gaming highlights how experimentation with tragic temporality—with choice in time—can challenge the assumption that time runs only in one direction, and, in Hotspur's words in Shakespeare's *1 Henry IV* that "time, that takes survey of all the world/Must have a stop" (5.4.82–3).[32] Performance and adaptation are inherently forms of repetition, with a difference[33]; in playing the actors always rise again, and the play begins anew, where one small change could make all the difference. Some time-travel films realize for the spectator and the character the hope that what you thought was the end was never really the end—or that there might be multiple ends. As I have explored throughout this book, the paradigm of the time loop, the redoing of the tragic present that embeds all forms of time, can also create the conditions of what feels like freedom of choice, even as we still operate, as Rosencrantz says, within limits.

On a bad day, one might take away from this discussion of videogames, time travel, and tragedy that there can be no real freedom in either of these contexts, whether it be within the enactment of the story as it has always been told, or in what Aarseth calls in "the prison-house of regulated play" (133). But I refuse to end this project on a pessimistic note. I am always cheered when I recall Céline's and Julie's inspired infiltration into that tragedy that is "toujours le même." Instead, I would like the reader to remember what I have come to appreciate about operating under present conditions of uncertainty: to embrace that uncertainty as much as I fear it. The traditions of tragedy have trained us to feel in every moment a sense of fatality about the end, rather than focusing on the possibilities of that moment. I understand the implications of everything that Rosencrantz means by limits—that there is no such thing as absolute freedom. But let us also try sometimes to transform the anxiety of present time's passing into the excitement of choosing to live through it.

NOTES

1. See, for example, Murray, *Hamlet on the Holodeck*; Juul, *Half-Real*; Juul, *The Art of Failure*; Bogost, *How to Do Things with Videogames*; Bogost, *Persuasive Games*; Gee, *What Videogames Have Teach Us*; Bissell, *Extra Lives*; Wolf and Bair, eds, *The Medium of the Videogame*; Schrank, *Avant-Garde Videogames*; Galloway, *Gaming*; and Wolf and Perron, eds. *The Video Game Theory Readers 1 and 2*.
2. The exception to this is Brenda Laurel's *Computers as Theatre*: This book is mostly focused on applying ideas from theater (including Aristotelian concepts) to the design of the "human-computer interaction" (Laurel 2014).
3. General studies of temporality include Nitsche, Mapping Time; Juul, Introduction to Game Time; Zagal and Mateas, Time in Videogames, and Moran, Playing with Game Time.
4. See Juul "Introduction to Game Time" on the difference between play time and event time (Juul 2006).
5. As Juul describes the difference: "Whereas action sequences have play time mapped to event time, cut scenes disconnect play time from event time" (135) (Juul 2006).
6. Homan and Homan have argued that this is "crucial to establishing real emotional connections between the gamer and his [sic] onscreen representative" (179) (Homan and Homan 2014).
7. On "time pressure and ticking clocks," see Wolf, *Medium of the Video Game*, Chap. 4. He notes that many games actually have ticking clocks while others mix "unlimited time with situations in which time is limited" (89) (Wolf 2001).

8. Some games such as *Dragon Age* do also allow for "real time with pause," in which time can be stopped for a player to prepare weapons or an attack strategy.

9. In a blog entry, Becky Chambers comments on how this choice mechanism works in another game produced by Tell-Tale Games, *The Walking Dead*: "Dialogue choices usually have to be made within seconds, or you'll lack the ability to make them at all. Spend too much time tugging your hair over a decision, and the other characters will take the conversation elsewhere, just as real people would. It's nerve-wracking, no doubt, especially when the choices at hand involve emotionally-fraught things like life, death, and (gulp) makeshift trauma surgery" ("Thoughts," Chambers 2015).

10. In an email communication of May 26, 2016 Ruth Toner brought to my attention "the recent massive resurgence in popularity of 'Rogue-like' games. They tend to be more gameplay than narrative focused, but these are essentially games where you only get one life, and if you mess up, you must start over with an entirely new character. There is no save reloading, so every decision you make must be carefully considered. Again, this is mostly done via gameplay (*Spelunky, The Binding of Isaac*, etc.)—if the enemy kills you, you're dead—but there are at least a few games which also do this with story."

11. See Hanson, 209 (Hanson 2014); see also Moran (2000).

12. See https://en.wikipedia.org/wiki/List_of_games_containing_time_tra vel. For example, the game *Prince of Persia: The Sands of Time* involves the story of a unnamed Persian prince who seizes a "dagger of time" that gives him the power to rewind time for ten seconds if he makes a mistake or dies (in addition to the player's ability to return to a checkpoint). However, the broader narrative also implies that the whole story is an exercise in time travel. The princess who is the prince's companion and love interest dies in a cut scene, but at the very end she is in fact alive and the prince tells her the game's story, presumably so the tragedy can be avoided in a newly created future.

13. *Life is Strange* quite consciously explores the theme of time through the media of film and photography. As reviewer Mike Futter notes: "For instance, you'll see double exposure when [Max is] rewinding time, along with different celluloid effects and even film burning as she tries to go too far backward" (Futter 2015).

14. Sicart also notes the function of hard choices in multiplayer games where reloading is not possible (Sicart 2013).

15. Mawhorter et al. specify the following categories for choice in games: dead-end option (ending the story); false choice (where all the options lead to the same end); blind choice (one without sufficient information); dilemma;

"flavor choice" (which affects the game world but not the end); delayed act; puzzle choice; and an "unchoice" (Mawhorter et al. 2014).

16. Alexa Ray Corriea comments on how the morality of *The Wolf Among Us* is affected by the viewpoint of a female character, Snow White: "Bigby is offered increasingly difficult choices that place his humanity on the line as the episodes continue. How much of himself, of his human self, will Bigby have to give up to earn respect from his fellow Fables? To solve the crimes and set things straight? And as we struggle with Bigby to retain his humanity despite dealing with some truly despicable characters, we measure his success in keeping it against Snow's reactions. She is our moral compass, our barometer for how much of Bigby is left. We see ourselves through her eyes" (Corriea 2013).

17. In the following discussion I will be referring to how character formation works in *Mass Effect 2*: while there are commonalities, there are also differences among the three parts of the trilogy.

18. Becky Chambers comments: "So often, story decisions are influenced (even if only slightly) by who we want to keep in our parties, what gear sets we want, what skill points we want to focus on. Popularity meters affect how much vendors will charge, or whether guards will attack on sight. Even when choices affect little but the flavor of the story or available dialogue, they're usually still coded in some way (Renegade/Paragon, Charisma/Dignity/Ferocity, etc.). This tells us that our decisions fit into clear-cut categories. For the most part, moral decisions are quantifiable" ("Thoughts," Chambers 2015).

19. The system in *Mass Effect* is actually far more complicated than this simple summary suggests: see http://masseffect.wikia.com/wiki/Morality. Accessed June 22, 2015.

20. Some videogame theorists have written about this function in the context of embodied cognition: so, for example, Karen Collins has observed "it is easy to conceive of the game controller as becoming an extension of the body"; we do not view the controller as part of our body but we can experience the virtual world by using it to "bump into walls, get shot, dig holes, and talk to other characters" (42–43) (Collins 2011). That extension of the body can provide both a sense of limitation and power. In *Prince of Persia: Sands of Time* not only does the player gain the power to control time, but also when the controls are mastered, she experiences the sensations of the avatar's acrobatic abilities, transcending what the ordinary human body can do. In this sense, the avatar is another form of cyborg, an association made explicit in a game like *Deus Ex: Human Revolution*, where the player constructs as an avatar Adam Jensen, a part-cyborg, by augmenting both his body and his social skills.

21. Mawhorter et al. distinguish between "avatar play" in which "you make choices as if you were your avatar" and "role play," where you make choices "based on what the focal character would do," though they acknowledge that it is often a hybrid (Mawhorter et al. 2014).

22. Gee relates how in playing the game *Arcanum*, he constructed a female "Half-Elf" avatar he named "Bead-Bead." Once race and gender are chosen, the game partially defines Bead-Bead's character, but then through the distribution of points the player further develops the character's nature. Like McCalmont, Gee reflects on how his own "nature" became transferred to his avatar, where his own physical failures can, for example, cause "Bead Bead to lose a fight against a weaker creature she could have otherwise beaten" or "fail to find his (Bead Bead's) way into a maze because he has poor spatial abilities (a trait Bead-Bead therefore inherits)" (57) (Gee 2014). On "projective embodiment," see also Holmes.

23. See Smethurst and Craps on the "trauma" of playing games (Smethurst and Craps 2015).

24. On *Heavy Rain* endings see http://heavyrain.wikia.com/wiki/Endings.

25. See http://www.ign.com/wikis/heavy-rain/Endings_Guide on ways to produce other endings once the game has been played through once.

26. Jake Gaskill continues in his account of this interview: "Of course, in the end, it is a game, and Cage understands that people will naturally want to go back and play through again, and even perhaps reload a previous save point to avoid unpleasant results that might occur because of actions taken in the game. To this, Cage says, 'I'm fine with that, but the right way to enjoy *Heavy Rain* is really to make one thing because it's going to be your story. It's going to be unique to you. It's really the story you decided to write [...] I think playing it several times is also a way to kill the magic of it'" (Gaskill 2009).

27. See also Smethurst and Craps: "The third aspect of games mentioned previously—complicity—is founded on a combination of interreactivity and empathy. Simply put, due to the unique ways in which players engage with them, games have the capability to make the player feel as though they are complicit in the perpetration of traumatic events" (277) (Smethurst and Craps 2015).

28. As Peter Parrish has commented in an interesting on-line conversation about choice and fate in the game, "*BioShock Infinite* is a game *about* choice, not a game *of* choice" (Parrish 2013).

29. See Wikipedia article on cheating in videogames for full coverage of different sort of cheating and how game designers have both contributed to and defended themselves against cheats of various kinds. https://en.wikipedia.org/wiki/Cheating_in_video_games.

30. Meades is primarily concerned with multiplayer games; see also *Fibreculture*'s special issue on counterplay: *Fibreculture* 16 (2010).
31. In an email communication of May 26, 2016 Ruth Toner shared the following observation about the game *Spec Ops*. "One of the most talked-about scenes regarding choice (or rather lack thereof) and morality in recent games is the famous 'White Phosphorus' scene in *Spec Ops: The Line*. The game is a stealth criticism of modern *Call of Duty* style shooters, and at one point, you can only proceed forward by setting off a White Phosphorus bomb, which (it is then revealed) kills a group of civilians. Here's an article discussing it: http://www.pcgamer.com/now-playing-spec-ops-most-troubling-scene/. "As the article says, many have commented that really, it's the game making the choice for you, and that the only way to make the 'right' decision is to stop playing the game altogether."
32. See Wagner 1–2 (Wagner 2014).
33. For a summary of ideas about performance and repetition, see Reinelt and Roach, 457–8 (Reinelt and Roach 2007).

BIBLIOGRAPHY

12 Monkeys. Dir. Terry Gilliam. Universal Pictures, 2009. Blu-ray.

Aarseth, Espen. I Fought the Law: Transgressive Play and the Implied Player. *DiGRA '07: Proceedings of the 2007 DiGRA International Conference: Situated Play.* http://www.digra.org/wp-content/uploads/digital-library/07313.03489.pdf. Accessed 02 April 2016.

Aeschylus. *Septem Quae Supersunt Tragoedias,* ed. Denys Page. Oxford: Oxford University Press, 1972. Print.

Altman, Rick. *Film/Genre.* London: British Film Institute, 1999. Print.

Apter, Emily. 'Women's Time' in Theory. *Difference* 21:1 (2010): 1–18.

Aristotle. *Poetics; Longinus: On the Sublime; Demetrius: On Style,* trans. Stephen Halliwell and Donald A. Russell. Loeb Classical Library 199. Revised edition. Cambridge, MA: Harvard University Press, 1995. Print.

Armstrong, Paul. *Play and the Politics of Reading: The Social Uses of Modernist Form.* Ithaca: Cornell University Press, 2002. Print.

Armstrong, Paul. *How Literature Plays with the Brain: The Neruoscience of Reading and Art.* Baltimore: Johns Hopkins University Press, 2013. Print.

Back to the Future. Dir. Robert Zemeckis. Universal Studios, 1985. DVD.

Bareham, Tony, ed. *Tom Stoppard: Rosencrantz and Guildenstern Are Dead, Jumpers and Travesties.* London: Palgrave Macmillan, 1989. Print.

Barker, Francis. *The Tremulous Private Body: Essays on Subjection.* 2nd edn. Ann Arbor: University of Michigan Press, 1995. Print.

Baumlin, James S., and Baumlin, Tita French. Chronos, Kairos, Aion: Failures of Decorum, Right-Timing and Revenge in Shakespeare's *Hamlet.* In *Rhetoric and Kairos: Essays in History, Theory, and Praxis,* eds. Phillip Sipora and James. S Baumlin. Albany: State University of New York Press, 2002. 165–186. Print.

© The Author(s) 2016

R. Bushnell, *Tragic Time in Drama, Film, and Videogames,*

DOI 10.1057/978-1-137-58526-4

Beckett, Samuel. *Waiting for Godot: A Tragicomedy in Two Acts*. New York: Grove Press, 1954. Print.

Belsey, Catherine. *The Subject of Tragedy: Identity and Difference in Renaissance Drama*. London: Methuen, 1985. Print.

Benjamin, Walter. *The Origins of German Tragic Drama*, trans. John Osborne. London: NLB, 1977. Print.

Berlin, Normand. *Rosencrantz and Guildenstern Are Dead*: Theater of Criticism. *Modern Drama* 16:3–4 (1973): 269–277.

Bernstein, Charles. Play it Again, Pac-Man. In *The Medium of the Video Game*, eds. Mark J.P. Wolf and Ralph H. Baer. Austin: University of Texas Press, 2002. 155–168. Print.

BioShock Infinite. PlayStation 3. Irrational Games, 2013. Videogame.

Bissell, Tom. *Extra Lives: Why Video Games Matter*. New York: Vintage, 2010. Print.

Blau, Herbert. *The Audience*. Baltimore: The Johns Hopkins University Press, 1990. Print.

Blind Chance. Dir. Krzysztof Kieslowski. 1981. Kino Video, 2004. DVD.

Bloom, Gina. Videogame Shakespeare: Enskilling Audiences Through Theater Making Games. *Shakespeare Studies* 43 (2015): 114–127.

Boal, Augusto. *Theatre of the Oppressed*, trans. Charles A. McBride. New York: Theatre Communication Group, 2001. Kindle.

Bogost, Ian. *Persuasive Games: The Expressive Power of Videogames*. Cambridge, MA: The MIT Press, 2010. Print.

Bogost, Ian. *How to Do Things with Videogames*. Minneapolis: University of Minnesota Press, 2011. Print.

Booth, Paul. 'Harmonious Synchronicity' and *Eternal Darkness*: Temporal Displacement in Video Games. In *Time Travel in Popular Media: Essays on Film, Television, Literature and Video Games*, eds. Matthew Jones and Joan Ormond. Jefferson, NC: McFarland & Company, 2015. 134–148. Print.

Bordwell, David. Film Futures. *SubStance* 31:1 (2002): 88–104.

Bordwell, David and Kristin Thompson. *Film: An Introduction*, 4th edn. New York: McGraw-Hill, 1992. Print.

Bradby, David. *Waiting For Godot*. Plays in Production. Cambridge: Cambridge University Press, 2001. Print.

Bradley, A. C. *Shakespearean Tragedy: Lectures on Hamlet, Othello, King Lear* and *Macbeth*, 2nd edn. London: Macmillan, 1924. Print.

Braid. PlayStation 3. Number None. 2009. Videogame.

Brecht, Bertolt. *Brecht on Theatre: The Development of an Aesthetic*, eds. Steve Giles and March Silberman, trans. John Willett. New York: Hill and Wang, 1977. Print.

Brook, Peter. *Reading for the Plot: Design and Intention in Literature*. New York: Knopf, 1984. Print.

Bryant, John. Textual identity and adaptive revision: Editing adaptation as a fluid text. In *Adaptation Studies: New Challenges, New Directions*, eds. Jørgen Bruhn, Anne Gjelsvik, and Eirik Frisvold Hanssen. London: Bloomsbury, 2013. Print.

Burges, Joel, and Elias, Amy J., eds. *Time: A Vocabulary of the Present*. New York: NYU Press, 2016. Kindle.

Burns, Edward. *Character: Acting and Being on the Pre-Modern Stage*. New York: St. Martins, 1990. Print.

Bushnell, Rebecca W. *Prophesying Tragedy: Sign and Voice in Sophocles' Theban Plays*. Ithaca: Cornell University Press, 1988. Print.

Bushnell, Rebecca W. Time and History in Early English Classical Drama. In *Law, Literature, and the Settlement of Regimes. Proceedings of the Folger Institute Center for the History of British Political Thought*, ed. Gordon Schochet. Vol. 2. Washington, DC: Folger Institute, 1990. 73–86.

Bushnell, Rebecca W. Tragedy and Temporality. *PMLA* 129 (2014): 783–789.

Caillois, Roger. *Man, Play and Games*, trans. Meyer Barash. Urbana and Chicago: University of Illinois Press, 2001. Print.

Calderwood, James. *Hamlet: The Name of Action. Modern Language Quarterly* 39 (1978): 331–362.

Cardwell, Sarah. About Time: Theorizing Adaptation, Temporality, and Tense. *Literature/Film Quarterly* 31:2 (2003): 82–92.

Carlson, Marvin. *Theatre Semiotics: Signs of Life*. Bloomington: Indiana University Press, 1990. Print.

Causey, Matthew. *Theatre and Performance in Digital Culture: From Simulation to Embeddedness*. London: Routledge, 2007. Print.

Cavell, Stanley. *Disowning Knowledge: In Seven Plays of Shakespeare*. Cambridge: Cambridge University Press, 2003. Print.

Céline and Julie Go Boating (Céline et Julie vont en bateau). Dir. Jacques Rivette. 1974. British Film Institute. DVD.

Chambers, Becky. "Everything You Need to Know About the Mass Effect 3 Ending Controversy, As Spoiler-Free As Possible." *The Mary Sue*. 20 March 2012. http://www.themarysue.com/everything-you-need-to-know-about-the-mass-effect-3-ending-controversy-as-spoiler-free-as-possible/. Accessed July 2015.

Chambers, Becky. "Laying Down My Sword: How Games Can Inspire Moral Decisions, Even Without Asking." 18 January 2013. *The Mary Sue*. http://www.themarysue.com/laying-down-my-sword-how-games-can-inspire-moral-decisions-even-without-asking/. Accessed 20 May 2015.

Chambers, Becky. "Thoughts On The Walking Dead, The Wolf Among Us, And Morality Systems (Or A Lack Thereof)." *The Mary Sue*. 19 May 2015. http://www.themarysue.com/telltale-games-morality-systems/. Accessed 6 June, 2016.

Chanter, Tina, and Sean D. Kirkland, eds. *The Returns of Antigone: Interdisciplinary Essays.* Albany: State University of New York Press, 2014. Print.

"Cheating in Video Games." *Wikipedia: The Free Encyclopedia.* N.d. Accessed 26 June 2015.

Cohen, Jeffrey J. *Medieval Identity Machines.* Minneapolis: University of Minnesota Press, 2003. Kindle.

Colie, Rosalie L. *The Resources of Kind,* ed. Barbara K. Lewalski. Berkeley: University of California Press, 1974. Print.

Collins, Karen. Making Gamers Cry: Mirror Neurons and Embodied Interaction with Game Sound. *Proceedings of the 6th Audio Mostly Conference: A Conference on Interaction with Sound.* New York: ACM, 2011. 39–46. *ACM Digital Library.* Accessed 23 July 2015.

Corriea, Alexa Ray. "The Female Gaze: How Being Watched Affects Morality in Adventure Games." *Polygon.* Vox Media, April 19, 2013. http://www.polygon.com/2014/4/9/5594270/the-female-gaze-how-being-watched-affects-morality-in-adventure-games. Accessed 6 June, 2016.

Costikyan, Greg. *Uncertainty in Games.* Reprint edition. Cambridge, MA: The MIT Press, 2013. Kindle.

Dahlen, Chris. "Game Designer Jonathan Blow: What We All Missed About Braid." *A.V. Club.* Onion, Inc., August 27, 2008. http://www.avclub.com/article/game-designer-jonathan-blow-what-we-all-missed-abo-8626. Accessed 20 May 2015.

Dasgupta, Gautam. Interview with Dominique Labourier and Juliet Berto. *Film* 2:24 (March 1975). Reprinted in the booklet accompanying the British Film Institute's DVD of *Céline and Julie Go Boating,* 2006.

De Grazia, Margreta. *"Hamlet" without Hamlet.* Cambridge: Cambridge University Press, 2007. Print.

De Romilly, Jacqueline. *Time in Greek Tragedy.* Ithaca: Cornell University Press, 1968. Print.

Déjà Vu. Dir. Tony Scott. Touchstone Pictures and Jerry Bruckheimer Films, 2006. DVD.

Del Rio, Elena. The Remaking of *La Jetée*'s Time Travel Narrative: *Twelve Monkeys* and the Rhetoric of Absolute Visibility. *Science Fiction Studies* 28:3 (2001): 383–398.

Deleuze, Gilles. *Cinema 2: The Time-Image,* trans. Hugh Tomlinson and Robert Galeta. Minneapolis: University of Minnesota Press, 1989. Print.

Deren, Maya. Cinematography: The Creative Use of Reality. In *Critical Visions in Film Theory,* eds. Timothy Corrigan and Patricia White with Meta Mazaj. Boston: Bedford/St. Martin's, 2011. 143–153. Print.

Derrida, Jacques. The Law of Genre, trans. Avital Ronell. *Critical Inquiry* 7 (1980): 55–81.

Deus Ex: Human Revolution. PlayStation 3. Square Enix. 2011. Videogame.

Dimock, Wai Chee. *Through Other Continents: American Literature Across Deep Time*. Princeton: Princeton University Press, 2006. Print.

Dimock, Wai Chee. Genres as a Field of Knowledge. *PMLA* 122:5 (2007): 1377–1388.

Dinshaw, Carolyn. *How Soon is Now?: Medieval Texts, Amateur Readers, and the Queerness of Time*. Durham: Duke University Press, 2012. Kindle.

DiPietro, Cary, and Grady, Hugh. eds. *Shakespeare and the Urgency of Now: Criticism and Theory in the 21ˢᵗ Century*. London: Palgrave Macmillan, 2013. Print.

Doane, Mary Ann. *The Emergence of Cinematic Time: Modernity, Contingency, the Archive*. Cambridge, MA: Harvard University Press, 2002. Print.

Dobin, Howard. *Merlin's Disciples: Prophecy, Poetry and Power in Renaissance England*. Palo Alto: Stanford University Press, 1990. Print.

Donlan, Christian. The Stanley Parable Review. *Eurogamer.net*. October 17, 2013. http://www.eurogamer.net/articles/2013-10-17-the-stanley-parable-review. Accessed 1 May 2016.

Donnie Darko: The Director's Cut. Dir. Richard Kelly. Twentieth Century Fox, 2004. Blu-Ray.

Dostal, Robert. Time and Phenomenology in Husserl and Heidegger. In *The Cambridge Companion to Heidegger*, ed. Charles B. Guignon. Cambridge: Cambridge University Press, 2006. 120–148.

Dubrow, Heather. *Genre*. London: Methuen, 1982. Print.

Eden, Kathy. Aristotle's *Poetics*: A Defense of Tragic Fiction. In *A Companion to Tragedy*, Ed. Rebecca Bushnell. Oxford: Blackwell, 2005. 41–50.

"Endings." *Heavy Rain Wiki*. N.d. http://heavyrain.wikia.com/wiki/Endings. Accessed 20 Jan. 2016.

"Ending Guide." *Heavy Rain*. http://www.ign.com/wikis/heavy-rain/Endings_Guide. Accessed 01 October 2016.

Euripides. *The Complete Euripides: Volume IV: Bacchae and other Plays*, eds. Peter Burian and Alan Shapiro. Oxford: Oxford University Press, 2009.

Evans, Owen. Tom Tykwer's *Run Lola Run*: Postmodern, Posthuman or 'Post-Theory'? *Studies in European Cinema* 1 (2004): 105–115.

Everett, Barbara. *Hamlet*: A Time to Die. *Shakespeare Survey* 30 (1977): 117–124.

Falk, Dan. *In Search of Time: The History, Physics and Philosophy of Time*. New York: Thomas Dunne Books/St. Martin's Griffin, 2010. Print.

Felski, Rita. Context Stinks. *New Literary History* 42:4 (2011): 573–591.

Fenner, James. "The Stanley Parable Endings Guide: the Definitive Ending Tree." *Guardian Liberty Voice*. Oct. 27, 2013. http://guardianlv.com/2013/10/the-stanley-parable-endings-guide-the-definitive-ending-tree/. Accessed 10 May 2016.

Fletcher, Angus. *Time, Space, and Motion in the Age of Shakespeare*. Harvard: Harvard University Press, 2007. Print.

Freshwater, Helen. *Theatre and Audience.* Basingstoke: Palgrave Macmillan, 2009. Print.

Frow, John. *Genre,* 2nd edn. Abingdon and NewYork: Routledge, 2015. Print.

Frye, Northrop. *Fools of Time: Studies in Shakespearean Tragedy.* Toronto: University of Toronto Press, 1967. Print.

Fuchs, Elinor. *The Death of Character: Perspectives on Theater after Modernism.* Bloomington: Indiana University Press, 1996. Print.

Furby, Jacqueline. Control Dramas and Play Time: Tales of Redemption and the Temporal Fantasist. In *Time Travel in Popular Media: Essays on Film, Television, Literature and Video Games,* eds. Matthew Jones and Joan Ormrod. Jefferson, N.C: McFarland & Company, 2015. 77–91. Print.

Futter, Mike. "Life is Strange." In *Game Informer.* GameStop, 23 January 2015. https://www.gameinformer.com/games/life_is_strange/b/pc/default.aspx. Accessed 6 June 2016.

Gallagher, Catherine. Undoing. In *Time and the Literary,* eds. Karen Newman, Jay Clayton, and Marianne Hirsch. New York: Routledge, 2002. 11–29. Print.

Galloway, Alexander R. *Gaming: Essays on Algorithmic Culture. Electronic Meditations.* Vol. *18.* Minneapolis: University of Minnesota Press, 2006. Kindle.

Garber, Marjorie. 'What's Past is Prologue': Temporality and Prophecy in Shakespeare's History Plays. In *Renaissance Genres: Essay on Theory, History, and Interpretation,* ed. Barbara Kiefer Lewalski. Harvard English Studies 14. Cambridge: Harvard University Press, 1986. 301–331.

Garber, Marjorie. *Shakespeare and Modern Culture.* New York: Pantheon, 2008. Print.

Gaskill, Jake. "Quantic Dream's David Cage: Play Heavy Rain Several Times, 'Kill the Magic of It.'"*G4TV.* G4 Media, August 31, 2009. http://www.g4tv.com/thefeed/blog/post/698809/quantic-dreams-david-cage-play-heavy-rain-several-times-kill-the-magic-of-it/. Accessed 2 April 2016.

Gee, James Paul. *What Video Games Have to Teach Us About Learning and Literacy,* 2nd edn. London: Palgrave Macmillan, 2014. Print.

Genette, Gérard. *Narrative Discourse: An Essay in Method,* trans. Jane E. Lewin. Ithaca: Cornell University Press, 1980. Print.

Gilbert, Helen and Joanne Tompkins. *Post-colonial Drama: Theory, Practice, Politics.* London: Routledge, 1996. Print.

Gladwell, Malcolm. *Blink: The Power of Thinking Without Thinking.* London: Back Bay Books, 2007. Print.

Goldstein, Hilary and Erik Brudvig. *"Mass Effect*: The Paragon and the Renegade." *IGN.* Ziff Davis, 7 November 2007. http://www.ign.com/articles/2007/11/08/mass-effect-the-paragon-and-the-renegade. Accessed 2 April 2016.

Gomel, Elana. Shapes of the Past and the Future: Darwin and the Narratology of Time Travel. *Narrative* 17:3 (2009): 334–352. Print.

Goodkin, Richard. Neoclassical Dramatic Theory in Seventeenth-Century France. In *A Companion to Tragedy*, ed. Rebecca Bushnell. Oxford: Blackwell, 2005. 373–392. Print.

Grene, David. *Reality and the Heroic Pattern: Last Plays of Ibsen, Sophocles, and Shakespeare*. Chicago: University of Chicago Press, 1967. Print.

Gruber, William E. 'Wheels within wheels, etcetera': Artistic Design in 'Rosencrantz and Guildenstern Are Dead'. *Comparative Drama* 15:4 (1981–1982): 291–310.

Hall, Edith, Fiona Macintosh, and Amanda Wrigley, eds. *Dionysus Since 69: Greek Tragedy at the Dawn of the Third Millennium*. Oxford: Oxford University Press, 2004. Print.

Hanson, Christopher. Repetition. In *The Routledge Companion to Video Game Studies*, eds. Mark J. P Wolf and Bernard Perron. New York: Routledge, 2014. 204–210. Print.

Harbord, Janet. *Chris Marker: La Jetée*. London: Afterall Books, 2009. Print.

Harris, Jonathan Gil. *Untimely Matter in the Time of Shakespeare*. Philadelphia: University of Pennsylvania Press, 2011. Print.

Heavy Rain. Playstation 3. Director's Cut. Quantic Dream. 2009. Videogame.

"Heavy Rain Trophy Guide." *Playstation Trophies*. N.d. http://www.playstation trophies.org/game/heavy-rain/guide/. Accessed 6 June, 2016.

Henderson, Diana. *Collaborations with the Past: Reshaping Shakespeare across Time and Media*. Ithaca: Cornell University Press, 2006. Print.

Herman, Arthur. *The Cave and the Light: Plato and Aristotle and the Struggle for the Soul of Western Civilization*. New York: Random House, 2013. Kindle.

Hirsh, James E. *The Structure of Shakespearean Scenes*. New Haven: Yale University Press, 1981. Print.

Hoffman, Piotr. Death, Time, History: Division II of *Being and Time*. In *The Cambridge Companion to Heidegger*, ed. Charles B. Guignon, 2nd edn. Cambridge: Cambridge University Press, 2006. 122–267. Print.

Holmes, Jeff. "Projective Embodiment in Videogames and Digital Spaces." *GAMERhetor*. 12 August 2014. https://gamerhetor.com/author/gamerhe tor/. Accessed 18 June 2016.

Homan, Daniel, and Sidney Homan. The Interactive Theater of Video Games: The Gamer as Playwright, Director, and Actor. *Comparative Drama* 48:1 (2014): 169–186.

Hoy, David Couzens. *The Time of Our Lives: A Critical History of Temporality*. Cambridge, MA: The MIT Press, 2012. Print.

Hutcheon, Linda and Siobhan O'Flynn. *A Theory of Adaptation*, 2nd edn. London: Routledge, 2013. Print.

Hutchinson, G.O. Sophocles and Time. In *Sophocles Revisited: Essays Presented To Sir Hugh Lloyd-Jones*, Oxford: Oxford University Press, 1999. 47–72. Print.

Jauss, Hans Robert. *Towards an Aesthetic of Reception*, trans. Timothy Bahti. Minneapolis: Univ. of Minnesota Press, 1982. Print.

Jones, John. *On Aristotle and Greek Tragedy*. Oxford: Oxford University Press, 1968. Print.

Jones, Matthew, and Joan Ormrod, eds. *Time Travel in Popular Media: Essays on Film, Television, Literature and Video Games*. Jefferson, N.C: McFarland & Company, 2015. Print.

Juul, Jesper. The Game, the Player, the World: Looking for a Heart of Gameness. Keynote presented at the Level Up conference in Utrecht, November 4th-6th 2003. https://www.jesperjuul.net/text/gameplayerworld/. Accessed 18 June 2016.

Juul, Jesper. *Half-Real: Video Games between Real Rules and Fictional Worlds*. Cambridge, MA: The MIT Press, 2005. Print.

Juul, Jesper. Introduction to Game Time. In *First Person: New Media as Story, Performance, and Game*, eds. Noah Wardrup-Fruin and Pat Harrigan. Cambridge, MA: MIT Press, 2006. 131–142. Print.

Juul, Jesper. *The Art of Failure: An Essay on the Pain of Playing Video Games*. Cambridge, MA: The MIT Press, 2013. Print.

Kahneman, Daniel. *Thinking, Fast and Slow*. New York: Farrar, Straus and Giroux, 2011. Print.

Kastan, David Scott. *Shakespeare and the Shapes of Time*. Hanover, N.H: University Press of New England, 1982. Print.

Kawin, Bruce. Time and Stasis in *La Jetée*. *Film Quarterly* 36:1 (1982): 15–20.

Kermode, Frank. Introduction to *Hamlet*. In *The Riverside Shakespeare*, ed. G. Blakemore Evans. New York: Houghton Mifflin, 1974. 1135–1140. Print.

Kermode, Frank. *The Sense of an Ending: Studies in the Theory of Fiction with a New Epilogue*. Oxford: Oxford University Press, 2000. Kindle.

Keyssar-Franke, Helene. The Strategy of 'Rosencrantz and Guildenstern Are Dead'. *Educational Theatre Journal* 27:1 (1975): 85–97.

Kidnie, Margaret Jane. Where is *Hamlet*? Text, Performance, and Adaptation. In *A Companion to Shakespeare and Performance*, eds. Barbara Hodgdon and W.B. Worthen. Oxford: Blackwell, 2005. 101–120.

Kidnie, Margaret Jane. *Shakespeare and the Problem of Adaptation*. London: Routledge, 2008. Print.

Kirkland, Sean D. Tragic Time. In *The Returns of Antigone: Interdisciplinary Essays*, eds. Tina Chantel and Sean. D. Kirkland. Albany: State University of New York Press, 2014. 51–68. Print.

Knox, Bernard M.W. *The Heroic Temper: Studies in Sophoclean Tragedy*. Berkeley: University of California Press, 1974. Print.

Knox, Bernard M.W. *Oedipus at Thebes: Sophocles' Tragic Hero and His Time*. New Haven: Yale University Press, 1998. Print.

La Jetée. Dir. Chris Marker. 1963. In *La Jetée /Sans Soleil.* Criterion Collection, 2007. DVD.

Landon, Brooks. *The Aesthetics of Ambivalence: Rethinking Science Fiction Film in the Age of Electronic (Re)production.* Westport, CT: Greenwood Press, 1992. Print.

Last Year at Marienbad. Dir. Alain Resnais. 1961. Criterion Collection, 2009. DVD.

Laurel, Brenda. *Computers as Theatre*, 2nd Edn. Upper Saddle River: Pearson, 2014. Print.

Lavender, Andy. *Hamlet in Pieces: Shakespeare Reworked by Peter Brook, Robert Lepage, Robert Wilson.* New York: Continuum, 2001. Print.

Leitch, Thomas. The Ethics of Infidelity. In *Adaptation Studies: New Approaches*, eds. Christa Albrecht-Crane and Dennis Cutchins. Madison, N.J. Fairleigh Dickinson University Press, 2010. 61–77. Print.

Levinson, Julie. Céline and Julie Go Story Telling. *The French Review* 65:2 (1991): 236–246.

Levy, Eric. *Hamlet and the Rethinking of Man.* Madison N.J.: Fairleigh Dickinson University Press, 2008. Print.

Lewis, Sarah. Shakespeare, Time, Theory. *Literature Compass* 11:4 (2014): 246–257.

Life is Strange. PlayStation 3. Square Enix. 2015. Videogame.

"List of Games Containing Time Travel." *Wikipedia: The Free Encyclopedia.* N.d. Accessed 4 May 2015.

Live Die Repeat: Edge of Tomorrow. Dir. Doug Liman. Warner Home Video, 2014. Blu-ray.

Loewenstein, George, Daniel Read, and Roy F. Baumeister. *Time and Decision: Economic and Psychological Perspectives on Intertemporal Choice.* New York: Russell Sage Foundation, 2003. Print.

Looper. Dir. Rian Johnson. Sony Pictures, 2012. Blu-ray.

Low, Jennifer A. and Nova Myhill, eds. *Imagining the Audience in Early Modern Drama, 1558–1642.* Basingstoke: Palgrave Macmillan, 2011.

Macdonald, Julia. Demonic Time in *Macbeth. Ben Jonson Journal* 17:1 (2010): 76–96.

Maisano, Scott. Now. In *Early Modern Theatricality*, ed. Henry S. Turner. Oxford: Oxford University Press, 2013. 368–385. Print.

Marchitello, Howard. Speed and the Problem of Real Time in *Macbeth. Shakespeare Quarterly* 64:4 (2013): 425–448.

Marlowe, Christopher. *Doctor Faustus: A and B Texts (1604, 1616).* eds. David Bevington and Eric Rasmussen. Manchester: Manchester University Press, 1993. Print.

Marvin, Carlson. *Theatre Semiotics: Signs of Life.* Advances in Semiotics. Bloomington: Indiana University Press, 1990. Print.

Mass Effect Trilogy. PlayStation 3. Bioware. 2012. Videogame.

Matz, Jesse. Aesthetic/Prosthetic. In *Time: A Vocabulary of the Present,* eds. Joel Burges and Amy J. Elias. New York: NYU Press, 2016. Kindle.

Maus, Katherine Eisaman. *Inwardness and Theater in the English Renaissance.* Chicago: University of Chicago Press, 1995. Print.

Mawhorter, Peter, Michael Mateas, Noah Wardrip-Fruin, and Arnav Jhala. Towards a Theory of Choice Poetics. *Proceedings of the 9th International Conference on the Foundations of Digital Games.* April 3–7 2014. Ft. Lauderdale, FL. https://games.soe.ucsc.edu/sites/default/files/choice-poetics-fdg-2014-camera-ready-v2.pdf. Accessed 23 September, 2014.

Mazer, Cary M. *Double Shakespeares: Emotional-Realist Acting and Contemporary Performance.* Madison: Fairleigh Dickinson University Press, 2015. Print.

McCalmont, Jonathan. "*Heavy Rain*: Free Will and Quick Time Events." *Futurismic.* 02 February 2011. http://futurismic.com/2011/02/02/heavy-rain-free-will-and-quick-time-events/. Accessed 2 April 2016.

Meades, Alan F. *Understanding Counterplay in Video Games.* New York: Routledge, 2015. Print.

Meeker, Joseph W. *The Comedy of Survival: Studies in Literary Ecology.* New York: Scribner, 1972. Print.

Morality. http://masseffect.wikia.com/wiki/Morality. Accessed 01 October 2016.

Moran, Chuck. Playing with Game Time: Auto-Saves and Undoing Despite the 'Magic Circle'. *The Fibreculture Journal* 16 (2000): http://sixteen.fibreculturejournal.org/playing-with-game-time-auto-saves-and-undoing-despite-the-magic-circle/. Accessed 2 April 2016.

Morson, Gary Saul. *Narrative and Freedom: The Shadows of Time.* New Haven: Yale University Press, 1996. Print.

Mulvey, Laura. The Index and the Uncanny. In *Time and the Image,* ed. Carolyn Bailey Gill. Manchester: Manchester University Press, 2000. 139–148. Print.

Murray, Janet H. *Hamlet on the Holodeck: The Future of Narrative in Cyberspace.* New York: The Free Press, 1997. Republished by The MIT Press, 1998. Print.

Nahin, Paul J. *Time Machines: Time Travel in Physics, Metaphysics, and Science Fiction.* New York: American Institute of Physics, 1993. Print.

Navarro-Remesal, Victor, and García-Catalán, Sheila. Try Again: The Time Loop as a Problem-Solving Process in *Save the Date* and *Source Code.* In *Time Travel in Popular Media: Essays on Film, Television, Literature and Video Games,* eds. Matthew Jones and Joan Ormrod. Jefferson, N.C: McFarland & Company, 2015. 206–218. Print.

Newman, Karen, Jay Clayton, and Marianne Hirsch, eds. *Time and the Literary.* New York: Routledge, 2002. Print.

Nitsche, Michael. Mapping Time in Video Games: Situated Play. *Proceedings of DiGRA* 2007 *Conference*, 145–151. http://sixteen.fibreculturejournal.org/playing-with-game-time-auto-saves-and-undoing-despite-the-magic-circle/. Accessed 18 June 2019.

Nussbaum, Martha. *The Fragility of Goodness: Luck and Ethics in Greek Tragedy and Philosophy*, 2nd edn. Cambridge: Cambridge University Press, 2001. Print.

Ohannessian, Kevin. "A Conversation With 'Heavy Rain' Creator David Cage Continues [Spoilers]." *Fastcocreate*. Fast Company, N.d. https://www.fastcocreate.com/1679015/a-conversation-with-heavy-rain-creator-david-cage-continues-spoilers. Accessed 1 May 2015.

Ohannessian, Kevin. "'Heavy Rain' Creator David Cage Reveals the Secrets of His Photo-Realistic Serial-Killer PS3 Game." *Fastcocreate*. Fast Company, 23 Feb. 2010. https://www.fastcocreate.com/1679014/heavy-rain-creator-david-cage-reveals-the-secrets-of-his-photo-realistic-serial-killer-ps3-g. Accessed 20 Jan. 2016

Orr, David. *The Road Not Taken: Finding America in the Poem Everyone Loves and Almost Everyone Gets Wrong*. New York: Penguin, 2015. Kindle.

Palfrey, Simon. *Shakespeare's Possible Worlds*. Cambridge: Cambridge University Press, 2014. Print.

Parrish, Peter. "The Bird, or the Cage: What BioShock Infinite Says about Choice and Fatalism." *PC Invasion*. April 6, 2013. http://www.pcinvasion.com/the-bird-or-the-cage-what-bioshock-infinite-says-about-choice-and-fatalism. Accessed 26 June 2015.

Penley, Constance. Time Travel, Primal Scene, and the Critical Dystopia. *Camera Obscura* 15 (1986): 67–84.

Performance Group, The *Dionysus in 69*, ed. Richard Schechner. New York: Farrar, Strauss and Giroux, 1970. Print.

Phillips, Tom. "BioShock Infinite Ending Explained." *Eurogamer.net*. April 4, 2013. http://www.eurogamer.net/articles/2013-04-04-bioshock-infinite-ending-explained. Accessed 02 April 2016.

Prince of Persia: The Sands of Time. PlayStation 2. Ubisoft Entertainment. 2009. Videogame.

Purchese, Robert. "*Life is Strange*: It Takes Time to be Different." *Eurogamer.net*. 09 December 2014. http://www.eurogamer.net/articles/2014-09-10-life-is-strange-it-takes-time-to-be-different. Accessed 02 April 2016.

Quinones, Ricardo J. *The Renaissance Discovery of Time*. Cambridge, MA: Harvard University Press, 1972. Print.

Raman, Shankar. Interrupted Games: Pascal, *Hamlet*, Probability. *Shakespeare Studies* 43 (2015): 179–207.

Rayner, Alice. *To Act, To Do, To Perform: Drama and the Phenomenology of Action*. Ann Arbor: University of Michigan Press, 1994. Print.

Reinelt, Janelle G., and Joseph R. Roach. *Critical Theory and Performance*. Revised and enlarged edition. Ann Arbor: University of Michigan Press, 2007. Print.

Richardson, Brian. 'The Time is Out of Joint': Narrative Models and the Temporality of the Drama. *Poetics Today* 8 (1987): 299–309.

Ricoeur, Paul. *Time and Narrative*. 3 vols. Chicago: University of Chicago Press, 1990. Print.

Riley, Alexander. *Impure Play: Sacredness, Transgression, and the Tragic in Popular Culture*. Plymouth: Lexington Books, 2010. Print.

Robbins, Bruce. Afterword. *PMLA* 122 (2007): 1644–1651.

Rodowick, D. N. Reading the Figural. *Camera Obscura* 24 (1990): 11–45.

Romney, Jonathan. *Céline and Julie Vont en Bateau*: Phantom Ladies over Paris. *International Dictionary of Films and Filmmakers*. 2001. *Encyclopedia.com*. http://www.encyclopedia.com/movies/dictionaries-thesauruses-pictures-and-press-releases/celine-et-julie-vont-en-bateau-phantom. Accessed 9 June 2016.

Rosenmeyer, Thomas G. *The Masks of Tragedy: Essays on Six Greek Dramas*. Austin: University of Texas Press, 2013. Print.

Rozett, Martha Tuck. *Talking Back to Shakespeare*. Newark: University of Delaware Press, 1994. Print.

Ruby, Jay, ed. *Crack in the Mirror: Reflexive Perspectives in Anthropology*. Philadelphia: University of Pennsylvania Press, 1982. Print.

Run Lola Run (Lola rennt). Dir. Tom Tykwer. Sony Pictures, 1999. DVD.

Sack, Daniel. *After Live: Possibility, Potentiality, and the Future of Performance*. Ann Arbor: University of Michigan Press, 2015. Print.

Sanders, Julie. *Adaptation and Appropriation*. New York: Routledge, 2006. Print.

Sartre, Jean-Paul. *No Exit and Three Other Plays*, trans. Lionel Abel. New York: Vintage International, 1989. Kindle.

Schanzer, Ernest. Shakespeare and the Doctrine of the Unity of Time. *Shakespeare Survey* 28 (1975): 57–62.

Schechner, Richard. There's Lots of Time in *Godot*. *Modern Drama* 9:3 (1966): 268–276.

Schechner, Richard. *Environmental Theater*. New York: Applause Theatre & Cinema Books, 2000. Print.

Schechner, Richard. *Performance Theory*, 2nd revised edition. London: Routledge, 2003. Print.

Schechner, Richard, and Victor Turner. *Between Theater and Anthropology*. Philadelphia: University of Pennsylvania Press, 1985. Print.

Schlueter, June. *Dramatic Closure: Reading the End*. Madison, NJ: Fairleigh Dickinson Press, 1995.

Schrag, Calvin O. *The Self after Postmodernity*. New Haven/London: Yale University Press, 1999. Print.

Schrank, Brian. *Avant-garde Videogames: Playing with Technoculture*. Cambridge, MA: MIT Press, 2014. Kindle.

Scott, Tony. *Déjà Vu*. Buena Vista Home Entertainment, 2007. DVD.

Segal, Charles. *Dionysiac Poetics and Euripides' Bacchae*. Princeton: Princeton University Press, 1982. Print.

Segal, Charles. *Oedipus Tyrannus: Tragic Heroism and the Limits of Knowledge*. New York: Twayne, 1993. Print.

Serreau, Geneviève. *Histoire du 'nouveau théâtre.'* Paris: Gallimard, 1966. Print.

Serres, Michel. *Conversations on Science, Culture, and TIme: Michel Serres with Bruno Latour*. trans. Roxanne Lapidus. Ann Arbor: University of Michigan Press, 1995. Print.

Shakespeare, William. *The Riverside Shakespeare*. ed. G. Blakemore Evans. New York: Houghton Mifflin, 1974. Print.

Shakespeare, William. *The Norton Shakespeare: Tragedies*. ed. Walter Cohen, Stephen Greenblatt, Jean E. Howard, and Katharine Eisaman Maus. New York: W.W. Norton, 1997. Print.

Shakespeare, William. *Hamlet*. In The Arden Shakespeare, eds. Ann Thompson and Neil Taylor. 3rd series. London: Bloomsbury, 2016. Print.

Shakespeare, William. *Mr. William Shakespeares Comedies, Histories and Tragedies* [*First Folio 1623*]. Fascimile edition prepared by Helge Kökeritz. New Haven: Yale University Press, 1954. Print.

Sicart, Miguel. *Beyond Choices: The Design of Ethical Gameplay*. Cambridge, MA: The MIT Press, 2013. Print.

Sidney, Sir Philip. The Defence of Poesy. In *Sidney's 'The Defence of Poesy' and Selected Renaissance Literary Criticism*, ed. Gavin Alexander. New York: Penguin, 2004. 1–54. Print.

Sinfield, Alan. *Faultlines: Cultural Materialism and the Politics of Dissident Reading*. Berkeley: University of California Press, 1992. Print.

Sliding Doors. Dir. Peter Howitt. Intemedia, Mirage, Miramax, and Paramount, 1998. DVD.

Smethurst, Toby, and Stef Craps. Playing with Trauma: Interreactivity, Empathy, and Complicity in *The Walking Dead* Video Game. *Games and Culture* 10:3 (2015): 269–290.

Snyder, Susan. *The Comic Matrix of Shakespeare's Tragedies: Romeo and Juliet, Hamlet, Othello, and King Lear*. Princeton, N.J: Princeton University Press, 1979. Print.

Sommerstein, Alan. Tragedy and Myth. In *A Companion to Tragedy*, ed. Rebecca Bushnell. Oxford: Blackwell, 2005. 163–180. Print.

Sophocles. *Fabulae*, ed A.C. Pearson. Oxford: Oxford University Press, 1975. Print.

Sophocles. *The Three Theban Plays*, trans. Robert Fagles. New York: Viking Penguin, 1984.

Source Code. Dir. Duncan Jones. Vendome Pictures, 2011. Blu-Ray.

States, Bert O. *The Shape of Paradox: An Essay on Waiting for Godot*. Berkeley: University of California Press, 1978. Print.

Steigerwalt, Jennifer L. *Renaissance Performance Practices on Modern Stages.* Diss. Arizona State University, 2013.

Stoppard, Tom. *Rosencrantz and Guildenstern Are Dead.* New York: Grove Press, 1971. Print.

Sypher, Wylie. *The Ethic of Time: Structures of Experience in Shakespeare.* New York: Seabury Press, 1976. Print.

The Stanley Parable. Windows version. Galactic Café, 2013. Videogame.

The Wolf Among Us. PlayStation 3. Tell-Tale Games, 2014. Videogame.

Toulmin, Stephen, and June Goodfield. *The Discovery of Time.* Chicago: University of Chicago Press, 1965. Print.

Turner, Frederick. *Shakespeare and the Nature of Time: Moral and Philosophical Themes in Some Plays and Poems of William Shakespeare.* Oxford: Clarendon Press, 1971. Print.

Turner, Victor. Dramatic Ritual/Ritual Drama: Performative and Reflexive Anthropology. In *A Crack in the Mirror: Reflexive Perspective in Anthropology,* ed. Jay Ruby. Philadelphia: University of Pennsylvania Press, 1982a. 83–97. Print.

Turner, Victor. *From Ritual to Theatre: The Human Seriousness of Play.* New York: PAJ, 1982. Print.

Tykwer, Tom. *Run Lola Run:* Director's Statement. Sony Classics, 1999. https://fischerfilm.files.wordpress.com/2008/08/tykweronlola.pdf. Accessed 05 April 2016.

Vernant, Jean-Pierre, and Pierre Vidal-Naquet. *Myth and Tragedy in Ancient Greece,* trans. Janet Lloyd. 2nd edition. New York: Zone Books, 1988. Print.

Wachhorst, Wyn. Time-Travel Romance on Film: Archetypes and Structures. *Extrapolation* 25:4 (1984): 340–359.

Wagner, Matthew. *Shakespeare, Theatre, and Time.* New York: Routledge, 2014. Print.

Waller, Gary F. *The Strong Necessity of Time: The Philosophy of Time in Shakespeare and Elizabethan Literature.* The Hague: Mouton De Gruyter, 1976. Print.

Wardrip-Fruin, Noah, and Pat Harrigan. eds. *First Person: New Media as Story, Performance, and Game.* Cambridge, MA: The MIT Press, 2006. Print.

Wedel, Michael. Backbeat and Overlap: Time, Place, and Character Subjectivity in *Run Lola Run.* In *Puzzle Films: Complex Storytelling in Contemporary Cinema,* ed. Warren Buckland. Chichester: Wiley-Blackwell, 2009. 129–150. Print.

Wells, H. G. *The Time Machine,* ed. Patrick Parrinder. New York: Penguin, 2007. Print.

Whalen, Tom. *Run Lola Run* (review). *Film Quarterly* 53:3 (2000): 33–40.

Whitaker, Thomas R. *Fields of Play in Modern Drama.* Princeton, N.J: Princeton University Press, 1977. Print.

Whitaker, Thomas R. *Tom Stoppard.* London: Macmillan, 1983. Print.

White, Gareth. *Audience Participation in Theatre: Aesthetics of the Invitation.* Basingstoke: Palgrave Macmillan, 2013. Print.

Whitehead, Dan. *Braid. Eurogamer.net.* 08 June 2008. http://www.eurogamer. net/articles/braid-review. Accessed 13 June 2015.

Whitman, Cedric H. *Euripides and the Full Circle of Myth.* Cambridge, MA: Harvard University Press, 1974. Print.

Widzisz, Marcel Andrew. *Chronos on the Threshold: Time, Ritual, and Agency in the Oresteia.* Lanham: Lexington Books, 2012. Print.

Wittenberg, David. *Time Travel: The Popular Philosophy of Narrative.* New York: Fordham University Press, 2013. Print.

Wolf, Mark J.P., and Ralph H. Baer, eds. *The Medium of the Video Game.* Austin: University of Texas Press, 2001. Print.

Wolf, Mark J.P., and Bernard Perron, eds. *The Video Game Theory Reader.* New York: Routledge, 2003. Print.

Wolf, Mark J.P., and Bernard Perron, eds. *The Video Game Theory Reader 2.* New York: Routledge, 2008. Print.

Wolf, Mark J.P., and Bernard Perron, eds. *The Routledge Companion to Video Game Studies.* New York, NY: Routledge, 2014. Print.

Wood, David Houston. *Time, Narrative, and Emotion in Early Modern England.* Farnham, Surrey: Ashgate, 2013. Print.

Wood, Robin. Narrative Pleasure: Two Films of Jacques Rivette. *Film Quarterly* 35:1 (1981): 2–12.

Worthen, William B. *Shakespeare and the Authority of Performance.* Cambridge: Cambridge University Press, 1997. Print.

Worthen, William B. *Shakespeare and the Force of Modern Performance.* Cambridge: Cambridge University Press, 2003. Print.

X-Men: Days of Future Past. Dir. Brian Singer. 20th Century Fox, 2014. DVD.

Yachnin, Paul, and Jessica Slights. eds. *Shakespeare and Character: Theory, History, Performance and Theatrical Persons.* Basingstoke: Palgrave Macmillan, 2008. Print.

Zagal, José P., and Michael Mateas. Time in Video Games: A Survey and Analysis. *Simulation & Gaming* 41:6 (2010): 844–868.

Zeitlin, Froma. The Dynamics of Misogyny: Myth and Mythmaking in the Oresteia. *Arethusa* 11 (1978): 149–175.

Zeitlin, Froma. Dionysus in 69. In *Dionysus Since 69: Greek Tragedy at the Dawn of the Third Millenium,* eds. Edith Hall, Fiona Macintosh, and Amanda Wrigley. Oxford: Oxford University Press, 2004. 49–76. Print.

Index

© The Author(s) 2016
R. Bushnell, *Tragic Time in Drama, Film, and Videogames*,
DOI 10.1057/978-1-137-58526-4